Jun. 2014

Assessment Balance and Quality
An Action Guide for School Leaders

Third Edition

Steve Chappuis, Carol Commodore, and Rick Stiggins

PEARSON

Boston   Columbus   Indianapolis   New York   San Francisco   Upper Saddle River
Amsterdam   Cape Town   Dubai   London   Madrid   Milan   Munich   Paris   Montreal   Toronto
Delhi   Mexico City   Sao Paulo   Sydney   Hong Kong   Seoul   Singapore   Taipei   Tokyo

Project Coordinator: Barbara Fankhauser

Editor: Robert L. Marcum, editorbob.com

Cover Design: George Barrett

Book design and typesetting: Curtis Bay and Heidi Bay, Grey Sky Design

Portions of this text have been reprinted or adapted from *Classroom Assessment* for *Student Learning: Doing It Right—Using It Well*, by Rick Stiggins, Judy Arter, Jan Chappuis, and Steve Chappuis, Boston, MA: Pearson Education, 2006; and *Seven Strategies of Assessment* for *Learning*, by Jan Chappuis, Boston, MA: Pearson Education, 2009. Reprinted and adapted by permission.

ISBN-10: 0-13-254878-X
ISBN-13: 978-0-13-254878-6

10 9 8 7 6 5

Acknowledgements

This guide represents years of experience that has helped us (1) form our vision of excellence in assessment, and (2) understand how to help schools use assessment to improve student learning. Along the way we have benefited from others who have worked to understand sound assessment more clearly, who applied our ideas and shared successful implementation stories, and those who have helped us teach others about quality assessment. We wish to thank them all. Those who have helped us deepen our own understanding of quality assessment and school leadership include Paul Black and Dylan Wiliam and their associates in the Assessment Reform Group of the United Kingdom, Janet Barry, Anne Davies, Rick DuFour, Dan Duke, Linda Elman, Michael Fullan, Tom Guskey, John Hattie, Heidi Hayes-Jacobs, Jim Popham, Lorrie Shepard, and Ruth Sutton. In addition Carol S. Dweck, Martin V. Covington, Martin E. P. Seligman, Eric Jensen, and Rhona Weinstein have made an impact on our thinking.

Many leaders from schools and districts have allowed us to work with them over the years, which allowed us to see the changes in practice. Some of these leaders are Gerald Beyer, Shannon Murray, and Carole Witt Stark, of the Merrill Area Public Schools in Merrill, WI; Nancy Bradley, Lynne Devaney, and David Olson of the Dubuque Community Schools, IA; Scott James, Val Calvert, and the building administrators for the Platte County School District No. 1, WY; Bonnie Laugerman of Arrowhead Union School District in Hartland, WI; Jay Linksman of the Professional Development Alliance in Illinois; Dana Monogue and Lisa Barrett Sigler of the School District of Waukesha, WI; Bob Nielsen of Bloomington, IL; Steve Price of Middletown, OH; and Pat Rochewski of the Nebraska Department of Education. We thank most of all the teachers and administrators of the School District of Elmbrook, WI, who worked tirelessly to bring quality assessment practices into their classrooms.

We welcome once again the contributions made by freelance editor Robert L. Marcum, which improved the clarity of ideas and activities presented in this book. His enthusiasm for the subject, attention to detail, and understanding of the big picture helped to unify the work of three authors.

We believe that the vision-building and strategies for change we describe in this guide can lead any school district to excellence in assessment. We acknowledge the commitment of those who are willing to try.

The Pearson Assessment Training Institute Staff

March, 2010

Foreword

Leading schools and school systems is hard work. There never seems to be enough time to accomplish everything that could be done. There is always another phone call that could be made, another document that could be reviewed, or another colleague who could be counseled. Few principals and superintendents leave work at the end of the day content in the knowledge that they achieved all the items on their agenda. This realization prompts a question: If educational leaders rarely accomplish everything they would like to accomplish, why are some leaders more effective than others?

Put differently, principals and superintendents vary greatly in their effectiveness. Yet few of these leaders manage to do everything that is expected of them. So what makes the difference? The difference lies in what leaders choose to do—and what they choose not to do. Effective leadership is less a matter of getting the most things done than doing the things that matter the most. And what matters the most? The things that are related, directly and indirectly, to teaching and learning.

This basic "truth" has been driven home to me in my work with leaders charged with turning around low-performing schools (Duke, 2010; Duke, Tucker, Salmonowicz, & Levy, 2007). Show me a chronically low-performing school and I'll show you a school where the principal and many of the faculty have failed to devote sufficient time and energy to curriculum alignment, instructional improvement, and assessments that support learning. These are findings of which the authors of this Action Guide are well aware.

That curriculum, instruction, and assessment are inseparable is a verity that educators often express more than they observe. Failure to appreciate the interrelationship of these three pillars of sound schooling, according to these authors, is first and foremost a failure of leadership. When principals and superintendents are unable to distinguish sound instruction and assessment from substandard practice, the likelihood that teachers will value and implement effective practices is not great.

Many guides for educational leaders adopt a tone that is both chastising and patronizing. Leaders are blamed for poor practice and then given recipes that insult their intelligence. Not so with this Action Guide. The authors recognize that educational leaders are, by and large, a skilled and intelligent group of professionals who, unfortunately, received little or no training in sound practices, especially with regard to assessment. What they offer in this book, however, is not a recipe, but a roadmap. The authors are savvy enough to realize that schools vary greatly in terms of context, composition, and culture. What leaders need are some guideposts to let them know that they are headed in the right direction.

The guideposts offered in the Action Guide represent seven precepts of sound assessment. Each precept is translated into actions that can be taken to promote assessment practices that support teaching and learning. "Support" is the key. Too often, assessment is associated with reporting, not supporting.

I am especially pleased that the authors address the role of students in the assessment process. One precept, for example, stresses the student's role as assessor. Another precept focuses on the relationship between student motivation and successful learning.

As a former school administrator and someone who has spent 35 years preparing school leaders, I can testify to the practical value of this Action Guide. It is chock full of practical activities designed to enhance our understanding of sound assessment practice and illustrates how such practice is crucial to productive learning. So universally applicable are the principles upon which this work is based that it just might help professors of educational leadership improve their own assessment practices.

Daniel L. Duke

Professor of Educational Leadership

University of Virginia

References

Duke, D. L. (2010). *Differentiating school leadership: Facing the challenges of practice*. Thousand Oaks, CA: Corwin.

Duke, D. L., Tucker, P. D., Salmonowicz, M. J., & Levy, M. (2007). How comparable are the perceived challenges facing principals of low-performing schools? *International Studies in Educational Administration, 35*(1), 3–21.

Table of Contents

Acknowledgements..iii

Foreword...v

PART 1   Laying the Foundation...1

Working at the System Level..4

Seven Actions to Ensure Student Success...5

Supporting the Learning of the Leaders..5

Contents of This Action Guide...6

Part 1: Laying the Foundation...6

Part 2: Building the Vision..6

Part 3: The Path to Assessment Balance and Quality...7

Part 4: Required Skills for Assessment Balance and Quality...8

Part 5: Planning for Action...8

Additional Content...8

PART 2   Building the Vision...11

Vision Part 1: Balanced Assessment Systems...13

Classroom Assessment...16

Interim/Benchmark Assessment..18

Annual Testing...18

Vision Part 2: Accurate Assessment...19

Keys to Accuracy...19

Keys to Effective Use...21

Vision Part 3: Classroom Assessment *for* Student Learning...22

Assessment *for* Learning..23

Summary of the Vision...25

Activity 1: Reflecting on the Vision of Excellence in Assessment..27

Activity 2: Building a Vision of a Quality, Balanced Assessment Program.................................28

PART 3 The Path to Assessment Balance and Quality 41

Beginning Your School or District Self-Evaluation 44

Action 1: Balance Your Assessment System 44

Is Your Assessment System in Balance? 45

Deepening Your Understanding of Balanced Assessment Systems 48

Activity 3: Formative or Summative? 50

Activity 4: Conducting an Assessment Audit 52

Action 2: Refine Achievement Standards 55

What Is the Current State of Your Achievement Standards? 56

Deepening Your Understanding of Refined Standards 57

Action 3: Ensure Assessment Quality 62

Can You Ensure Assessment Quality? 62

Deepening Your Understanding of Assessment Quality 63

Action 4: Help Learners Become Assessors by Using Assessment *for* Learning
Strategies in the Classroom 66

Are Your Learners Involved in Their Own Assessment? 68

Deepening Your Understanding of Assessment *for* Learning Strategies in the Classroom 69

Action 5: Build Communication Systems That Both Support and Report Learning 73

Do Your Teachers Know How to Communicate Effectively about Student Learning? 74

Deepening Your Understanding of Balanced Communication Systems 74

Action 6: Motivate Students with Learning Success 76

Do Your Teachers Use Learning Success to Motivate Students? 78

Deepening Your Understanding of How to Motivate Students with Learning Success 78

Action 7: Promote the Development of Assessment Literacy 80

Do You Need to Promote the Development of Assessment Literacy? 82

Deepening Your Understanding of How to Promote Assessment Literacy 82

Summarizing the Path to Excellence in Assessment 83

Activity 5: School/District Assessment System Self-Evaluation 84

PART 4 Required Skills for Assessment Balance and Quality 95

Leading Assessment *for* Learning 97

Competency 1: The leader understands the attributes of a sound and balanced assessment system, and the conditions required to achieve balance in local systems..................100

Success Indicators for Competency 1 101

Practice with Competency 1...101

Activity 6: Merging Local and State Assessment Systems 101

Activity 7: Auditing for Balance in Classroom Assessment...................................103

Competency 2: The leader understands the necessity of clear academic achievement standards, aligned classroom-level achievement targets, and their relationship to the development of accurate assessments. 106

Success Indicators for Competency 2..107

Practice with Competency 2...108

Activity 8: Embracing the Vision of a Standards-based School 108

Activity 9: Implementing the Written Curriculum..109

Activity 10: Deconstructing Standards into Classroom-level Achievement Targets: Practice for School Leaders...113

Competency 3: The leader understands the standards of quality for student assessments, helps teachers learn to assess accurately, and ensures that these standards are met in all school/district assessments. 124

Success Indicators for Competency 3..126

Practice with Competency 3...126

Activity 11: Indicators of Sound Classroom Assessment Practice 126

Activity 12: Analyze Assessments for Clear Targets 129

Competency 4: The leader knows assessment *for* learning practices and works with staff to integrate them into classroom instruction.......................................133

Success Indicators for Competency 4..134

Practice with Competency 4...134

Activity 13: Communicating Learning Targets in Student-friendly Language...........134

Activity 14: Assessment for *Learning Self-evaluation* 138

Competency 5: The leader creates the conditions necessary for the appropriate use and reporting of student achievement information, and can communicate effectively with all members of the school community about student assessment results, including report card grades, and their relationship to improving curriculum and instruction......................141

Communicating Annual Test Scores to Parents and Community.............................141

Grading and Reporting...142

Success Indicators for Competency 5..143

Practice with Competency 5...144

Activity 15: A Rubric for Sound Grading Practice...144

Activity 16: When Grades Don't Match the State Assessment Results 149

Activity 17: A Standard Cover Letter to Parents...150

Competency 6: The leader understands the issues related to the unethical and inappropriate use of student assessment and protects students and staff from such misuse...........................153

Success Indicators for Competency 6...154

Practice with Competency 6..154

Activity 18: "Is This Responsible?" 155

Activity 19: Guidelines for Test Preparation and Administration 157

Competency 7: The leader can plan, present, and/or secure professional development activities that contribute to the use of sound assessment practices....................................160

Success Indicators for Competency 7...161

Practice with Competency 7..161

Activity 20: Supporting Teacher Learning Teams 162

Activity 21: Discussing Key Assessment Concepts with Faculty.............................171

Competency 8: The leader knows and can evaluate teachers' classroom assessment competencies, and helps teachers learn to assess accurately and use the results to benefit student learning...179

Success Indicators for Competency 8...180

Practice with Competency 8..181

Activity 22: Verifying Teachers' Content Knowledge and Assessment Competence....................181

Activity 23: Should Teachers Be Held Accountable for Assessment Competence through Evaluation? 183

Competency 9: The leader analyzes student assessment information accurately, uses the information to improve curriculum and instruction, and assists teachers in doing the same. 185

Common and Interim/Benchmark Assessments...186

Annual Assessments 186

Success Indicators for Competency 9...188

Practice with Competency 9..188

Competency 10: The leader develops and implements sound assessment and assessment-related policies...189

Success Indicators for Competency 10...191

Practice with Competency 10...191

Activity 24: Using School/District Policies to Support Quality Assessment................................191

Activity 25: A Self-analysis for School Leaders..197

PART 5   Planning for Action 199

Activity 26: Making Connections between Leadership Competencies and the
Seven Actions...202

Activity 27: Making Connections between a District's Current Direction and
Assessment Literacy...204

Activity 28: Linking the Ten Assessment Competencies for School Leaders with
the 2008 ISLLC Educational Leadership Policy Standards and the Twenty-one
Principal Leadership Responsibilities...206

Action Planning for Assessment Balance and Quality...209

Where Are We Trying to Go with Our Assessment System?...209

Where Are We Now?...209

How Can We Close the Gap between the Two? 209

Prioritizing the Actions to Take...210

Action Planning Templates..211

Top Section of the Action Planning Template 211

Bottom Section of the Action Planning Template 212

Additional Planning Considerations..216

The Comprehensive Assessment Plan 216

Helping Policy Makers Understand Balance and Quality..216

Communicating and Monitoring the Plan 217

Analysis of Impact 217

Case Study of an Individual Teacher or a Few Teachers 218

The Study of a Learning Team 218

In Closing 219

References 221

About the Authors 225

CD-ROM/DVD Contents... 227

Laying the Foundation

STUDENT
SUCCESS

Teacher
Competencies

Planning
for
Action

Required Skills
for Assessment
Balance and Quality

The Path to Assessment
Balance and Quality

Building the Vision

Laying the Foundation

The Building Blocks of Assessment Success

Laying the Foundation

1

To succeed in standards-based school improvement we must be clear about what students need to know and be able to do, and we need to be skillful in how we teach. To be certain that students have learned what we intend for them to learn, we must develop balanced assessment systems that provide data on how students are progressing, systems that also use the classroom assessment process to promote even greater learning. What we teach, how we teach it, how well we assess, and how we use assessment to improve student achievement will all determine the success of our efforts, and ultimately, how we are judged.

Today's standards-based environment is a very different one from when the focus was on effective schools research, when instructional leadership and teacher supervision were common topics in principal training programs. Today, with school improvement taking on more urgency due to federal, state, and local accountability requirements and the resulting need to raise test scores, improving leadership knowledge and skill is being leveraged as one more strategy directly aimed at raising student achievement.

Evidence suggests that the culture we create in our schools can positively influence student success. Collaborative cultures emphasizing teamwork and continuous learning and improvement are positioned to deliver the sustained professional support teachers need, support aimed at demonstrable results in student achievement. And the role of the leader continues to be studied, with scholars and practitioners alike working to translate research into practice, describing what effective leadership looks and sounds like. The number of websites, books, articles, and conferences devoted to the subject of school leadership makes it clear that part of the success equation for schools is in the office of the principal. Research evidence shows the difference effective school leaders can have on student learning (Leithwood, Louis, Anderson, & Wahlstrom, 2004; Waters, Marzano, & McNulty, 2003). Leaders must be focused not only on what to improve, but also on how to engender the institutional changes necessary for greater student success (Davidovich, Nikolay, Laugerman, & Commodore, 2010). This focus requires a dual mindset of consistency and innovation (Fullan, 2008).

This focus on the role and effectiveness of the school leader provides new understandings about the nature of leadership, and is in part influenced by thinking outside of education. Earlier contributions from business management (Covey, 1989; Peters

& Waterman, 1982; Senge, 1990) and from human psychology/motivation (Blanchard & Johnson, 1982) are joined by current thinking and insight (Collins, 2001; Gladwell, 2000; Goleman, Boyatzis, & McKee, 2002). All share a common foundation in that they describe principles and values by which leaders can live and work, principles more complex than simply following a checklist of behaviors or practices applied in isolation from a set of core beliefs.

Historically we have sustained a set of beliefs about assessment's role in improving schools that does not promote success for all students. Given our new educational mission of helping all students master standards of learning, the time has come to examine those beliefs and determine if they are preventing us from using the assessment process to promote learning. If so, we need to adopt new beliefs that will drive assessment practices centered on student success. This calls for leaders who can lead their organizations through the exploration of a whole new set of assessment beliefs and practices. This guide details Seven Actions that leaders can take to complete that exploration and, in doing so, provide an assessment environment where all students will prosper, especially those who struggle to learn.

Working at the System Level

The current assessment reality for most school administrators is dominated by the need for students to demonstrate mastery of content standards on annual state assessments. This guide reflects our belief, backed by research, that quality assessment used effectively day to day in the classroom is integral to student success. Further, we believe that classroom assessment is a key part of the foundation both for school improvement and for standards-based teaching and learning, and is a key component in a balanced assessment system.

This guide provides a structure through which you as a district or school leader can do the following:

- Refine your vision of excellence in assessment for your school or district.
- Examine the beliefs, practices, knowledge, and actions needed to realize your vision.
- Make connections between quality assessment and your organization's mission, belief statements, and improvement plans.
- Develop an action plan to turn your vision into reality.

By using this guide in a local leadership study team with your colleagues, including district and building administrators and teacher leaders, you can achieve a balanced, instructionally relevant local assessment system in which classroom, interim/benchmark, and annual assessments can both support and verify learning. You can balance assessments *for* learning and assessments *of* learning effectively, ensuring they serve their intended purpose.

Seven Actions to Ensure Student Success

Developing an action plan for assessment balance and quality requires a local school or district to conduct a self-evaluation of its current assessment system. In this guide we provide a tool for this analysis based on how thoroughly the school or district has completed the following Seven Actions:

1. Balance the district's assessment system to meet all key user needs.

2. Refine achievement standards to reflect clear and appropriate expectations at all levels.

3. Ensure assessment quality in all contexts to support good decision making.

4. Help learners become assessors by using assessment *for* learning strategies in the classroom.

5. Build communication systems to support and report student learning.

6. Motivate students with learning success.

7. Provide the professional development needed to ensure a foundation of assessment literacy throughout the system.

Supporting the Learning of the Leaders

Beyond working at the systems level for achieving assessment balance and quality, this Action Guide also will help you as a school leader analyze your individual knowledge about assessment and can guide your continuing learning about sound assessment practices. By completing the work presented here, you will continue to develop your own assessment literacy. This guide will help you and your team do the following:

- Understand the need for an assessment system that is balanced, meeting the information needs of key users from the classroom, interim/benchmark, and annual testing levels.

- Understand the need for all assessments to be of high quality.

- Understand the beliefs and practices that must underlie a quality, balanced assessment program.

- Understand the Seven Actions that can bring quality and balance to local systems.

- Analyze the district's current status regarding completion of these actions.

- Develop a plan for completing the Seven Actions that will bring assessment excellence to the district and its classrooms.

- Understand classroom assessment *for* learning practices and their relationship to student achievement.

- Analyze your own assessment knowledge and leadership skills relative to a set of competencies for school leaders that are instrumental in completing the Seven Actions.

Contents of This Action Guide

Figure 1-1 shows the building blocks of assessment success. It also maps our journey through this Action Guide. To help you and your leadership team develop understanding of each of the building blocks, we've divided this book into five parts.

Part 1: Laying the Foundation

Part 1 introduces this guide's purpose and goals, describes both its print and media contents, and explains its use in the context of a school or district leadership study team.

We encourage the same model of professional development for this Action Guide that we advocate for teachers to become assessment literate. All it requires is a small group of school leaders willing to meet regularly and invest the necessary time in their own professional growth and in the improvement of their local system. By acquiring certain understandings, considering important issues, and planning for the future as a team, leaders demonstrate the commitment to learning sought in all aspects of school culture.

Part 2: Building the Vision

Part 2 assists you in building a vision for your assessment system. We outline our own vision and describe the foundation necessary to develop an assessment system rooted in balance, quality, and student involvement. We ask you to reflect on that vision to

Figure 1-1   **The Building Blocks of Assessment Success**

help further extend your concept of what your own assessment system should look like.

Part 2 also guides you in seeing the connections between your organization's current work and direction with that of quality assessment. Many districts and schools have established their mission/vision and have developed plans to make their mission/vision real in every classroom. But sometimes all of this work at all levels of the organization seems chaotic, disjointed, or sporadic. Assessment literacy is a powerful coherence maker (Fullan, 2001). Seeing the connections between what the district is already trying to accomplish and sound assessment practices can help stimulate and organize the district around its mission.

Part 3: The Path to Assessment Balance and Quality

Part 3 asks leadership teams to consider the Seven Actions that lead to a comprehensive assessment system. After introducing the Actions, we ask you to analyze your own system regarding its current status relative to each, then provide suggestions on how you can close the gap between where your self-evaluation shows you to be now and where you could be.

Part 4: Required Skills for Assessment Balance and Quality

In Part 4 we shift emphasis from analyzing organizational and institutional assessment excellence to examining the assessment knowledge and skills that individual leaders need. We also examine further the knowledge and skills needed by classroom teachers, and help school leaders see how they can support teachers in their professional development and ongoing classroom assessment practice.

Part 5: Planning for Action

In the fifth and final part we ask you to think about both your organizational analysis from Part 3 as well as your individual analysis from Part 4, and use them to create the action plan that will lead to assessment balance and quality in your school or district. We assist you in prioritizing actions and offer suggestions for evaluating your action plan both before and during its implementation.

Additional Content

From time to time, we will ask your team to pause to discuss and reflect on certain aspects of assessment and their implications for your school or district. We have included activities, all under the heading of "Thinking About Assessment," to help you consider, clarify, and use the ideas and strategies presented. For each activity we include the purpose, approximate time frames, needed materials, suggested room setups, and step-by-step directions. Some activities also include resource sheets, pages that can help your team prepare for and organize successful implementation of balanced assessment systems. Some are best suited for use with the leadership team; others can be used as faculty meeting or inservice activities with teachers.

CD and DVD

This guide also includes a CD-ROM and a DVD, found in plastic sleeves inside the back cover.

The CD-ROM contains reproducible copies of the activity descriptions and resource sheets, as well as tools for leaders to use with other educators when working through the assessment ideas and issues presented here.

The DVD, *Developing Balanced Assessment Systems: Seven Essential Actions for Schools and Districts*, features Dr. Rick Stiggins. In this 35-minute presentation, Dr. Stiggins describes and discusses each of the Seven Actions.

For Teachers: Classroom Assessment *for* Student Learning

This Action Guide is aimed at helping leaders understand what they can do to ensure balance and quality in local assessment systems. No doubt you already realize, however, that teachers play the pivotal role in using assessment to promote even greater student learning. The skills and knowledge teachers need, although introduced in this book for leaders, are not explicitly taught in this guide. The content we do introduce as central to what assessment-literate teachers do in the classroom is drawn primarily from *Classroom Assessment* for *Student Learning: Doing It Right—Using It Well* (Stiggins, Arter, Chappuis, & Chappuis, 2006) and *Seven Strategies of Assessment* for *Learning* (Chappuis, 2009).

10

PART

2

Building the Vision

STUDENT
SUCCESS

Teacher
Competencies

Planning
for
Action

Required Skills
for Assessment
Balance and Quality

The Path to Assessment
Balance and Quality

Building the Vision

Laying the Foundation

The Building Blocks of Assessment Success

Building the Vision

2

To achieve excellence in assessment at the local level district, school, and classroom leaders will need to team up to develop an integrated system that uses the assessment process and its results, both to verify student success and to support student learning. To do so requires (1) balancing assessment uses to serve a variety of purposes, (2) accurate assessments that yield dependable results and (3) developing a classroom assessment environment that involves students as partners in monitoring and managing their own success while they are learning.

A *balanced assessment system* satisfies the information needs of all assessment users at the classroom, building, and district levels. *Accurate assessments* provide these users with the evidence of achievement they need to do their jobs. We know that, to maximize learning, *students* must top the list of assessment users—assessment results must be shared with students and teachers, so they can participate in making key data-based instructional decisions. In Part 2 we explore each of these components to assist your leadership team in formulating its own vision of excellence in assessment. Once your team has created that local vision, you can evaluate where you are now in relation to where you want to be, and can plan your own strategies for closing the gap. Parts 3–5 of this guide will assist you with your self-study and action planning.

Vision Part 1: Balanced Assessment Systems

Assessment is, in part, the process of gathering evidence of student learning to inform instructional decisions. Local district assessment systems promote student success when they help to inform decisions that both support and verify learning; that is, when the system is designed to serve both *formative* and *summative* purposes across all relevant levels of assessment use.

These levels of use are (1) day-to-day *classroom* assessment, (2) periodic *interim/ benchmark* assessment, and (3) *annual* standardized testing. Table 2-1 crosses these three use levels with formative and summative applications to outline the integrated mission of a balanced system in terms of the full array of purposes it must serve. These purposes derive from the answers within each level to the following questions:

- What are the *key decisions* to be informed by assessment results?

- Who are the *decision makers*?

- What *information* do they need to make sound decisions?

- What essential *assessment conditions* must be satisfied to ensure they get that information?

In a balanced assessment system, the needed evidence flows into the hands of the intended decision maker(s) in a timely and understandable form. Please review Table 2-1 before continuing.

Table 2-1   **Framework for a Balanced Assessment System**

Level of Assessment/Key Issues	Formative Applications	Summative Applications
Classroom Assessment		
Key decision(s) to be informed?	What comes next in each student's learning?	What standards has each student mastered? What grade does each student receive?
Who is the decision maker?	Students and teachers	Teacher
What information do they need?	Evidence of where the student is now on learning continuum	Evidence of each student's mastery of each relevant standard
What are the essential assessment conditions?	• Appropriate standards in learning progressions • Accurate assessment results • Results leading to next steps • Results as descriptive feedback	• Clear and appropriate standards • Accurate evidence • Evidence well summarized • Grading symbols that carry clear and consistent meaning for all

Table 2-1 **Framework for a Balanced Assessment System** *(continued)*

Level of Assessment/Key Issues	Formative Applications	Summative Applications
Interim/Benchmark Assessment		
Key decision(s) to be informed?	Where can we improve instructional programs right away? Where are students struggling?	Did the program of instruction deliver as promised? Should we continue to use it?
Who is the decision maker?	Professional learning communities; district and building instructional leaders	Instructional leaders
What information do they need?	Standards students are struggling to master	Accurate evidence of student mastery of particular program standards
What are the essential assessment conditions?	• Clear and appropriate standards • Accurate assessment results • Results revealing how *each* student did in mastering *each* standard	Accurate assessments focused on specific program standards aggregated over learners
Annual Accountability Testing		
Key decision(s) to be informed?	Where and how can we improve instruction next year?	Are enough students meeting standards?
Who is the decision maker?	School leaders, curriculum & instructional leaders	School and community leaders
What information do they need?	Standards students are struggling to master	Percent of students meeting *each* standard
What are the essential assessment conditions?	Accurate evidence of how *each* student did in mastering *each* standard aggregated over students	Accurate evidence of how *each* student did in mastering *each* standard aggregated over students

Classroom Assessment

Two aspects of the *classroom* assessment level are worthy of note. The first is that, historically, it has been almost completely ignored as a school improvement tool. Over the decades, we as a nation have made immense investment in local, state, national, and international standardized testing, followed more recently by increased levels of standardized interim/benchmark testing. During this same period, we have invested almost nothing to ensure the quality or effective use of the other 99.9 percent of the assessments that happen in students' lives—those conducted day to day with their teachers in their classroom. Yet classroom assessment has proven its worth in enhancing achievement (Black & Wiliam, 1998). For this reason, *no assessment system can really be in balance unless the classroom level of assessment is fulfilling its role in supporting and verifying learning.*

Second, while classroom-level instructional decisions differ between formative and summative uses, the essential assessment conditions remain constant. Achievement standards must be spelled out from the beginning of instruction in the form of deconstructed, clear, and appropriate learning targets. Further, these learning targets must be turned into quality assessments that yield dependable information with sufficient precision to reflect how well each student mastered each of the standards. Only then can teachers and students know which standards have yet to be mastered (formative purposes), or the extent to which each student succeeded in meeting requirements (summative purposes).

As we have worked to promote effective classroom assessment, we have adopted labels introduced by an international community of educational researchers and practitioners. We refer to assessments that support and promote learning as "assessment *for* learning" and applications that verify or certify achievement as "assessment *of* learning." Both are important, but they are different, and effective local assessment systems balance the two. Table 2-2 compares them in terms of purposes, users, and other aspects. Thought of in a broad sense, assessment *for* learning is formative assessment that actively involves students in every aspect of their own assessment.

Table 2-2   **Comparing Assessment *for* and *of* Learning: Overview of Key Differences**

	Assessment *for* Learning	Assessment *of* Learning
Reasons for Assessing	Promote increases in achievement to help students meet more standards; support ongoing student growth; improvement	Document individual or group achievement or mastery of standards; measure achievement status at a point in time for purposes of reporting; accountability
Audience	Students about themselves	Others about students
Focus of Assessment	Specific achievement targets selected by teachers that enable students to build toward standards	Achievement standards for which schools, teachers, and students are held accountable
Place in Time	Process during learning	Event after learning
Primary Users	Students, teachers, parents	Policy makers, program planners, supervisors, teachers, students, parents
Typical Uses	Provide students with insight to improve achievement; help teachers diagnose and respond to student needs; help parents see progress over time; help parents support learning	Certify competence or sort students according to achievement for public relations, gatekeeper decisions, grading, graduation, or advancement
Teacher's Role	Transform standards into classroom targets; inform students of targets; build assessments; adjust instruction based on results; involve students in assessment	Administer the test carefully to ensure accuracy and comparability of results; use results to help students meet standards; interpret results for parents; teachers also build assessments for report card grading
Student's Role	Self-assess and contribute to setting goals; act on classroom assessment results to be able to do better next time	Study to meet standards; take the test; strive for the highest possible score; avoid failure
Primary Motivator	Belief that success in learning is achievable	Threat of punishment, promise of rewards
Examples	Using rubrics with students; student self-assessment; descriptive feedback to students	Achievement tests; final exams; placement tests, short-cycle assessments

Source: Adapted from *Understanding School Assessment* (pp. 17 & 18), by J. Chappuis and S. Chappuis, 2002, Portland, OR: Assessment Training Institute. Copyright 2006, 2002 by Educational Testing Service. Adapted by permission.

Interim/Benchmark Assessment

At the *interim/benchmark* level of assessment, formative use requires advance planning. In this case, assessments can be used periodically during the term to keep track of student progress in mastering each standard. Note that if these are to be used in formative ways (that is, to promote further learning), accountability or grading decisions should not come into play. The primary purpose should be to identify standards students are struggling to master and the students struggling to meet those standards. This allows teachers to use the results in two ways. First, it provides them the information needed to zero in on how to improve their own instruction aimed at those standards. Second, these results can help teachers and students focus on identifying student strengths and areas needing improvement so they can plan interventions together that overcome problems students may be experiencing individually or collectively.

On the summative side at this level the purpose is often to determine the viability of a particular educational program, however that is defined in your local context: should you continue or discontinue the instructional methodology, current text adoption, curricular sequence, and so on. To inform such judgments, the assessment must reflect the intended learning outcomes of that program.

Common Assessments

Many schools and districts around the country are forming professional learning communities (PLCs) (DuFour, DuFour, Eaker, & Karhanek, 2004). In PLCs, faculty who have the same teaching assignments collaborate to identify common learning targets, develop (or purchase) common assessments linked to those targets, conduct those assessments, and process results together to learn, in part, how they can improve student learning. When these assessments are properly focused on the targets of instruction and are of high quality, the results also can serve to highlight subsets of students within and across classrooms who have specific instructional needs. When this happens common assessments can inform classroom assessment–level instructional decisions, too. To help with this or with program improvement, the assessment results must tell users *how well each student mastered each standard.* Teachers can then use this level of information to focus their efforts to overcome specific student weaknesses.

Annual Testing

When it comes to *annual testing*, tradition has centered on summative accountability decisions: Did enough students succeed at mastering the standards? Is each school performing and producing successful students as it should be? But note once again in this context that for these questions to be answered, assessment results must provide a sufficiently high-resolution portrait of student learning to reveal how well each student mastered each standard. In other words, it is of little value to develop long lists of standards, assemble test items sampling broadly across that list, and set a total test score cutoff to determine if each student satisfied requirements defined as the total set of standards. At best, such an assessment will undersample the standards its items reflect; at worst, the assessment is likely to omit some standards. When this happens, inferences about individual student mastery of individual standards are indefensible.

Additionally, if the assessment is to tell you how well each student mastered each standard, then an important annual formative application becomes viable. As with the interim/benchmark level, you can aggregate results across students to identify which standards students struggled to master. You then can focus long-term program improvement efforts on those standards most in need of attention next year.

To summarize, a balanced assessment system relies on assessments from multiple levels that work together to inform decisions that both support and verify student learning. The questions for your leadership team to answer are, Are we in balance? Do we have in place an integrated set of assessments that can provide the information needed to help students succeed?

Vision Part 2: Accurate Assessment

Assessment users can make sound instructional decisions only if the data they rely on (the assessment results gathered) provide an accurate picture of the current level of student learning. Schools that go to the trouble to develop and administer more tests but then do not ensure the results will be accurate have the classic "garbage in, garbage out" situation. A faulty test results in faulty data, which, unfortunately, leads to faulty decisions about students. To ensure dependable results, teachers and school leaders need to learn how to develop and use assessments in ways that satisfy five key criteria for assessment quality (illustrated in Figure 2-1), each of which highlights a particular dimension of quality in the form of a continuum from weak to strong. Three criteria contribute to assessment accuracy, and two focus on their effective use. An initial overview follows.

Keys to Accuracy

Creating a quality assessment begins with clear answers to the questions, *Why* are we conducting this assessment? What is its purpose? How will the results be used? We

Figure 2-1 **Keys to Quality Classroom Assessment**

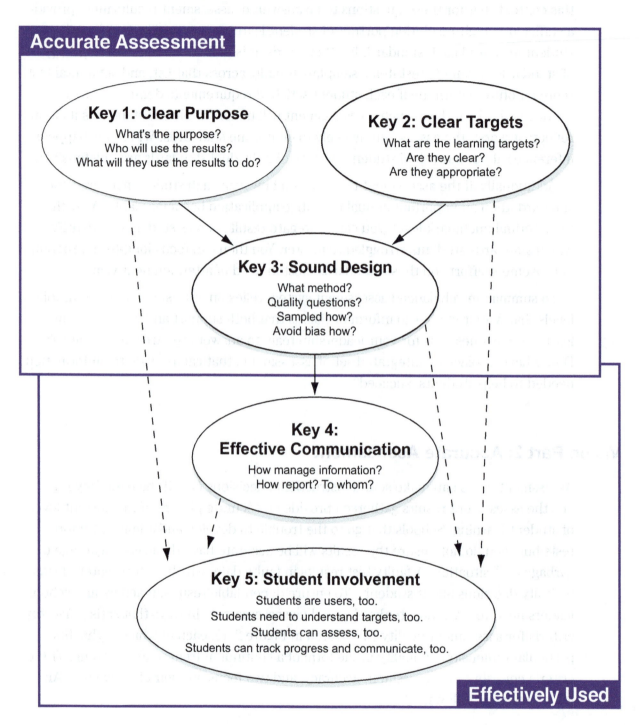

introduced this issue in the previous section. The developer must begin with a plan of who will use the results and how. What instructional decisions will be made? Without a sense of user(s) and use(s) of the assessment, the developer cannot infer what kind of information it must produce. How can one build an assessment to provide information without knowing what information is needed?

Assessment users can make sound instructional decisions only if the data they rely on (the assessment results gathered) provide an accurate picture of the current level of student learning.

As discussed previously, teachers can use classroom assessment to support learning, as an instructional intervention (assessment *for* learning), or to verify learning, as in assigning grades, for example (assessment *of* learning). The challenge is to be clear from the beginning of assessment development which purpose is being served.

The second question addressed in assessment development is, *What* student achievement is to be assessed? Without clear targets—an established set of achievement expectations to be taught and learned—the author cannot properly focus test items or scoring procedures. The assessment must measure student achievement of the intended learning.

Once the assessment purpose is defined and learning target(s) identified, then *assessment design* can begin. The creation of a quality assessment for any particular context requires the following:

- Selection of a proper assessment method

- Development of quality items, exercises, and scoring guides

- Proper sampling of student achievement so as to draw a proper inference about student learning success

- Elimination of relevant sources of bias that can distort results

Keys to Effective Use

A good assessment will yield sound evidence of student learning. The next challenge is to get the results into the hands of the intended user(s) so they can inform instructional decisions. This requires *effective communication*. The characteristics of good communication will vary depending on the formative or summative purpose of the assessment. Regardless, the highest-quality assessment yielding the most accurate results is wasted if its results are miscommunicated. We share guidelines for effective communication later in this guide.

The second key to effective assessment use centers on *students as users of assessment results*. When students become involved in the assessment process during their learning and have the opportunity to watch themselves improve over time, their confidence, motivation, and achievement also improve. This is "assessment *for* learning," and represents the third foundational concept to the development of a balanced local assessment system. Compelling evidence of the efficacy of assessment *for* learning is detailed in two comprehensive research reviews (Black & Wiliam, 1998; Hattie & Timperley, 2007).

Vision Part 3: Classroom Assessment *for* Student Learning

Black and Wiliam's (1998) review of research on the impact of formative assessment reveals profound achievement gains attributable to the effective management of the day-to-day classroom assessment process. Effective management includes providing students with clear learning targets, descriptive feedback, and intentionally involving students in the entire assessment process, including self-assessment, goal-setting, monitoring, and communicating results.

When students become involved in the assessment process during their learning and have the opportunity to watch themselves improve over time, their confidence, motivation, and achievement also improve.

Sadler (1989) provides an orientation to this way of thinking about classroom assessment by contending that the teacher's challenge is to help students understand (1) what good work looks like from the very beginning of the learning (know where I'm going), (2) how to compare their work to that standard of excellence such that the differences become clear to them (know where I am now), and (3) how to close the gap between them (know where and how to improve). Atkin, Black, & Coffey (2001) convert these understandings into three brief questions.

Chappuis (2009) blends these ideas into a series of seven assessment/instructional strategies that provide a useful framework for thinking about formative classroom assessment practices that involve students as active users of assessment information. Teachers must be provided with the opportunity to learn how to do the following (Chappuis, 2009, pp. 11–13):

Where Am I Going?

Strategy 1: Provide students with a clear and understandable vision of the learning target.

Strategy 2: Use examples and models of strong and weak work.

Where Am I Now?

Strategy 3: Offer regular descriptive feedback.

Strategy 4: Teach students to self-assess and set goals.

How Can I Close the Gap?

Strategy 5: Design lessons to focus on one learning target or aspect of quality at a time.

Strategy 6: Teach students focused revision.

Strategy 7: Engage students in self-reflection, and let them keep track of and share their learning.

Implicit in these seven strategies is an understanding of how important the student's role is as an assessment user, decision maker, and player in the entire assessment experience. In this paradigm students reflect on their own assessment results, interpreting their scores and grades to decide how to proceed, or if to proceed at all. If students decide to move on then the learning moves forward and the teachers/decision makers get to play their role on behalf of student success. But if learners decide that success is beyond reach then the others have no role to play and the learning stops.

The question is, What can teachers do to help students respond productively to every assessment? The answer is to consistently apply these strategies and principles of assessment *for* learning by helping students see where they are headed, where they are now, and how to close the gap. In doing so, teachers help students feel in control of the probability of their own success.

Assessment *for* Learning

Here's how it works: In an assessment *for* learning environment, students have continuous access to evidence of their own learning, and they collaborate with their teachers in understanding, based on the evidence, what comes next in that learning. Their success in moving forward turns on their emotional reaction to their assessment results. For successful learners, these issues tend to resolve themselves automatically and comfortably. Ongoing success spawns the actions needed to produce more success. But, for struggling learners, chronic failure can lead to a pattern of just giving up.

Historically, schools have served the mission of ranking students from the highest to the lowest achiever. The amount of time available to learn was fixed: one year per grade. The amount learned by the end of that time varied; some students learned a great deal, some very little. Able learners built on past success to grow rapidly. However, students who failed to master the early prerequisites within the allotted time also failed to learn what followed. In the schools of our youth, if we worked hard and learned a great deal, that was a positive result, as we would occupy places high in the rank order. And, if we gave up in the face of what we believed to be inevitable failure—that was an acceptable result for the institution too, because we would occupy places low in the rank order. The greater the spread of achievement from top to bottom, the more dependable the rank order.

The emotional dynamics of this process were clear and purposeful. From the very earliest grades, some students rode winning streaks to the top. Right from the start, they scored high on assessments and were assigned high grades. The emotional effect of this was that they came to see themselves as capable learners—they became increasingly confident in school. That gave them the emotional strength to risk striving for more success because in their minds success was within reach if they tried. Note that the trigger for the decisions they made about their own learning was *their interpretation of their own assessment results.*

But students who scored very low on tests right from the beginning were assigned correspondingly low grades. This caused them from the outset to doubt their own capabilities as learners. Their loss of confidence deprived them of the emotional reserves to continue to risk trying. Chronic failure was hard to hide and became embarrassing—it was better not to try. As their motivation waned, their achievement suffered. Notice again how the learners' own interpretation of assessment results influenced their confidence and willingness to strive on.

The important lesson educators must learn is that students' emotional reactions to any set of assessment results, whether high, midrange, or low, will determine what they think, feel, and do in response to those results.

The driving emotional forces of fear and intimidation triggered by the prospect of being held accountable now must be replaced by the driving emotions of optimism, engagement, and persistence triggered by the belief that "I am going to get this if I keep trying." If all students are to succeed, they must have continuous access to credible evidence of their own academic *success* at mastering prescribed achievement standards. Again, the Black and Wiliam (1998), Sadler (1989), Atkin, Black, and Coffey (2001), and Chappuis (2009) suggestions and lessons apply directly.

Under a new mission of not leaving any child behind, the teacher's objectives should now include helping students develop a strong sense of control over their own academic success. In terms of general psychology, Bandura (1994) refers to this sense as *self-efficacy*:

> A strong sense of efficacy enhances human accomplishment and personal well-being in many ways. People with high assurance in their capabilities approach difficult tasks as challenges to be mastered rather than as threats to be avoided. Such an efficacious outlook fosters intrinsic interest and deep engrossment in activities. They set themselves challenging goals and maintain strong commitment to them. They heighten and sustain their efforts in the face of failure. They quickly recover their sense of efficacy after failures or setbacks. They attribute failure to insufficient effort or deficient knowledge and skills which are acquirable. They approach threatening situations with assurance that they can exercise control over them. Such an efficacious outlook produces personal accomplishments, reduces stress and lowers vulnerability. . . .
>
> In contrast, people who doubt their capabilities shy away from difficult tasks which they view as personal threats. They have low aspirations and weak commitment to the goals they choose to pursue. When faced with difficult tasks, they dwell on their personal deficiencies, on the obstacles they will encounter, and all kinds of adverse outcomes rather than concentrate on how to perform successfully. They slacken their efforts and give up quickly in the face of difficulties. They are slow to recover their sense of efficacy following failure or setbacks. Because they view insufficient performance as deficient aptitude, it does not require much failure for them to lose faith in their capabilities. (p. 71)

In terms of classroom assessment competence, teachers can help students build a strong sense of academic self-efficacy by helping them understand what success looks like and then by showing them how to use information from each assessment to get closer and closer to the target. In these classrooms, assessments become far more than merely one-time events attached to the end of the teaching. They become part of the learning process by keeping students both posted on their progress and confident enough to continue striving. Later in this text we detail how to make sure this happens for all learners.

Summary of the Vision

The locus of control for the achievement of assessment balance and quality is the local school district, as this is the only level of the educational system at which assessment can serve valuable purposes at annual, interim/benchmark, and classroom levels. Neither federal nor state education agencies can use assessment to benefit student learning in all of the ways local schools can. This doesn't mean federal and state agencies can't contribute to and support local excellence in assessment. They can adopt policies that support assessment literacy and the use of classroom assessment to support student learning. They can also help keep "high stakes" annual tests in perspective—by being clear about their value and limitations.

The five Keys to Assessment Quality (see Figure 2-1) are integral to effective local assessment systems. District and school leaders must understand the conditions that are essential for assessment to work well in any context: a clear purpose for the assessment, clear and appropriate learning targets, and accurate, sound assessment design and delivery.

It also is important for school leaders and teachers to understand the benefits of involving students in their own formative assessment. Students, as the ones who actually choose whether to strive or give up, need to understand the learning targets clearly and know exactly where they are in relation to mastering those targets.

The final component is effective communication of results; for all involved to understand the diverse information needs of assessment users at all levels: students and teachers at the classroom level, teachers and curriculum leaders at the interim/benchmark level, and school leaders at the annual testing level. Excellence in assessment is achieved when all user questions are answered with the right information delivered in a timely and understandable form using high-quality assessments.

Thinking About Assessment

Activity 1: Reflecting on the Vision of Excellence in Assessment

Purpose:

As leaders part of your task is to share the vision of excellence with others and invite them in to further shape that vision and make it become a reality. This activity will help you clarify the main elements of a balanced assessment program.

Time:

30 minutes

Materials Needed:

The vision as presented in this guide

Suggested Room Setup:

Tables and chairs set up for easy discussion among those present

Directions:

Each of you has read Part 2 of this book, "Building the Vision." With your learning team members present, answer together the following questions so each member can share with others a vision for excellence in assessment.

1. Why is excellence in assessment necessary for improved student learning?

2. In the context of an integrated system that uses the assessment process and its results to both support and audit learning, what are the three active ingredients?

3. What does a balanced assessment system look like?

4. What are the five keys to assessment quality? Summarize each key in your own words.

5. Assessment *for* learning answers three questions students have when learning: Where am I going? Where am I now? How can I close the gap? Describe how Chappuis's (2009) seven strategies help students answer these questions.

Thinking About Assessment

Activity 2: Building a Vision of a Quality, Balanced Assessment Program

Purpose:

Having a vision of a balanced assessment program is essential to starting the journey of incorporating quality assessment practices in every classroom in your school or district. When you can articulate that vision it is easier to invite others in to shape it and own it.

The activity has two parts. In Part 1 you will draft in your own words a vision of a balanced assessment program that later you can share with others. Part 2 illustrates high-quality assessment in action in the lives of real students, teachers, administrators, and policy makers. You will revisit your vision of excellence in assessment and reaffirm or rethink and revise it.

Later in this Action Guide we ask your team to compare your current assessment program status to this new vision and identify what you must adjust to make it a reality.

PART 1

Time:

2 ½ hour meeting

Materials Needed:

- Blank index cards

- Flipchart paper and markers, easels if available

- Table 2-1, "Framework for a Balanced Assessment System," on pp. 14–15 of this Action Guide

Suggested Room Setup:

- Team members seated at tables of six to eight people

- Flipchart, easels if available, and markers for each table

Directions:

Table Discussion (30 minutes)

You have just read Part 2 of this book, "Building the Vision." Working as table teams, using Table 2-1 as a template and based on your current understanding of important assessment issues and systemic change, outline your vision of a high-quality assessment system. Brainstorm and refine your team's answers to the following two questions.

1. What do you want your assessment system to accomplish? What will be its key objectives?

2. How will your system accomplish these things? What will be its key components?

Use your flipchart paper to record your answers/ideas for shaping your preliminary vision (Figure 2-2). Post each team's ideas around the room.

Figure 2-2   **Building Your Vision: The "What" and "How" Table Discussion**

What do you want your assessment system to accomplish? What will be its key objectives?

How will you accomplish these things? What will be its key components?

First Gallery Walk (20 minutes):

Walk around and view the preliminary vision statements from the various tables. Note what you see as similarities and differences among the visions.

Return to your tables and share your findings. Decide as a team whether to revise your table's vision statement.

PART 2

Time:

40 minutes after reading and discussing Part 2 of this text

Materials Needed:

- "Emily's Story," found on pp. 32–39.
- Flipcharts from Part 1 of this activity containing each table's vision of a balanced assessment system
- Sheets of multicolored sticky dots for each team's table

Directions:

Read "Emily's Story," one student's experience with assessment *for* learning and the impact it had on her confidence as a learner.

1. Reflect on the keys to success for Emily and her classmates. Focus on the student and teacher strategies that brought confidence and responsibility to Emily as a learner.

2. Make note of the conditions that needed to be in place for Emily and her class-mates, Ms. Weathersby and her colleagues, school leaders, and the community to facilitate this success.

3. After reading "Emily's Story," engage in a team discussion centered around the following questions. We suggest that you read over these discussion questions before reading:

   — What strategies/activities were Emily and her classmates engaged in to bring success to them as learners?

   — What was Ms. W.'s role?

   — What was Emily's emotional response to these assessment experiences in her learning?

Brainstorm lists of those necessary conditions for Emily's success by answering the following questions:

- What conditions needed to be in place in Ms. W.'s classroom?

- What conditions needed to be in place in the English Department and the high school?

- What contribution did the district need to make for this success to happen?

- What contribution did the school board and community need to make?

As a leadership team, then, address the following questions:

- To what extent are these conditions satisfied in your classrooms, schools, district, and community?

- What might you need to change or add to your team's vision of assessment excellence as a result of reading this story? Make changes on your vision statements (flipchart paper).

Second Gallery Walk—A District Vision of a Quality, Balanced Assessment Program (30 minutes):

Again display your vision statements (flipchart paper) and as teams take a second gallery walk. Use the following process:

1. Take a sheet of colored dots from your table.

2. Go to each posted vision and place a dot next to an element/component that you believe must be addressed/included in the district vision statement for a quality, balanced assessment system.

3. Note what is common to the visions around the room.

4. Decide as a team whether elements that are not in common should be discussed in a large group, to consider if to include or exclude any of these elements and why.

Table Discussion (15 minutes) and Large-group Discussion (15 minutes):

Discuss your responses to process items 3 and 4 as a table and then as a large group. Come to a consensus on what components/elements your school or district vision for balanced assessment should have. Designate one person to keep a summary of the large-group discussion.

Select one representative from each table to take the dotted sheets and the large-group discussion summary and draft a common district vision of a quality, balanced assessment system. Return to the large group later in the day or on another day for final consensus on the elements and the wording. Note and discuss how this vision of assessment aligns with Table 2-1, "Framework for a Balanced Assessment System." on pp. 14–15 of this guide.

As the group works through Part 3 of this Action Guide, on the Seven Actions to high-quality assessment, and begins to grapple with the leadership competencies presented in Part 4 you will want to revisit your vision statement. During this time it will be a dynamic document subject to revisions based on your deepening understanding of balanced assessment and the process necessary to make it a reality in every classroom.

A STORY OF CLASSROOM SUCCESS

Emily's Story

A Vision of Success

At a local school board meeting, the English faculty from the high school presents the results of their evaluation of the new writing instruction program that they had implemented over the past year. The audience includes a young woman named Emily, a junior at the local high school, sitting in the back of the room with her parents. She knows she will be a big part of the presentation. She's only a little nervous. She understands how important her role is. It has been quite a year for her, unlike any she has ever experienced in school before. She also knows her parents and teacher are as proud of her as she is of herself.

As part of their preparation for this program, the English faculty attended a summer institute on assessing writing proficiency and integrating such assessments into their teaching and their students' learning. The teachers were confident that this kind of professional development and their subsequent program revisions would produce much higher levels of writing proficiency.

As the first step in presenting program evaluation results, the English department chair, Ms. Weathersby, who also happens to be Emily's English teacher, distributes a sample of student writing to the board members (with the student's name removed), asking them to read and evaluate this writing. They do so, expressing their dismay aloud as they go. They are less than complimentary in their commentary on these samples of student work. One board member reports with some frustration that, if these represent the results of that new writing program, the new program clearly is not working. The board member is right. This is, in fact, a pretty weak piece of work. Emily's mom puts her arm around her daughter's shoulder and hugs her.

But Ms. Weathersby urges patience and asks the board members to be very specific in stating what they don't like about this work. As the board registers its complaints, a faculty member records the criticisms on chart paper for all to see. The list is long, including everything from repetitiveness to disorganization to short, choppy sentences and disconnected ideas.

Next, Ms. Weathersby distributes another sample of student writing, asking the board to read and evaluate it. Ah, now this, they report, is more like it! This work is much better! But be specific, she demands. What do you like about this work? They list positive aspects: good choice of words, sound sentence structure, clever ideas, and so on. Emily is ready to burst! She squeezes her mom's hand.

The reason she's so full of pride at this moment is that this has been a special year for her and her classmates. For the first time ever, they became partners with their English teachers in managing their own improvement as writers. Early in the year, Ms. Weathersby ("Ms. W.," they all call her) made it crystal clear to Emily that she was, in fact, not a very good writer and that just trying hard to get better was not going to be enough. She expected Emily to improve—nothing else would suffice.

Ms. W. started the year by working with students to implement new state writing standards, including understanding quality performance in word choice, sentence structure, organization, and voice, and by sharing some new "analytical scoring guides" written just for students. Each scoring guide explained the differences between good and poor-quality writing in understandable terms. When Emily and her teacher evaluated her first two pieces of writing using these standards, she received very low ratings. Not very good. . . .

But she also began to study samples of writing Ms. W. provided that Emily could see were very good. Slowly, she began to understand why they were good. The differences between these and her work started to become clear. Ms. W. began to share examples and strategies that would help her writing improve one step at a time. As she practiced and time passed, Emily and her classmates kept samples of their old writing to compare to their new writing, and they began to build portfolios. Thus, she literally began to watch her own writing skills improve before her very eyes. At midyear, her parents were invited in for a conference at which Emily, not Ms. Weathersby, shared the contents of her portfolio and discussed her emerging writing skills. Emily remembers sharing thoughts about some aspects of her writing that had become very strong and some examples of things she still needed to work on. Now, the year was at an end and here she sat waiting for her turn to speak to the school board about all of this. What a year!

Now, having set the board up by having them analyze, evaluate, and compare these two samples of student work, Ms. W. springs a surprise. The two pieces of writing they had just evaluated, one of relatively poor quality and one of outstanding quality, were produced by the same writer at the beginning and at the end of the school year! This, she reports, is evidence of the kind of impact the new writing program is having on student writing proficiency.

Needless to say, all are impressed. However, one board member wonders aloud, "Have all your students improved in this way?" Having anticipated the question, the rest of the English faculty joins the presentation and produces carefully prepared charts depicting dramatic changes in typical student performance over time on rating scales for each of six clearly articulated dimensions of good writing. They accompany their description of student performance on each scale with actual samples of student work illustrating various levels of proficiency.

Further, Ms. W. informs the board that the student whose improvement has been so dramatically illustrated with the work they have just analyzed is present at this school board meeting, along with her parents. This student is ready to talk with the board about the nature of her learning experience. Emily, you're on!

Interest among the board members runs high. Emily talks about how she has come to understand the truly important differences between good and bad writing. She refers to differences she had not understood before, how she has learned to assess her own writing and to fix it when it doesn't "work well," and how she and her classmates have learned to talk with her teacher and each other about what it means to write well. Ms. W. talks about the improved focus of writing instruction, increase in student motivation, and important positive changes in the very nature of the student–teacher relationship.

A board member asks Emily if she likes to write, and she answers, "I do now!" This board member turns to Emily's parents and asks their impression of all of this. They report with pride that they had never seen so much evidence before of Emily's achievement and most of it came from Emily herself. Emily had never been called on to lead the parent-teacher conference before. They had no idea she was so articulate. They loved it. Their daughter's pride in and accountability for her achievement has skyrocketed in the past year.

As the meeting ends, it is clear to all in attendance that evening that this application of student-involved classroom assessment had contributed to important learning. The English faculty accepted responsibility for student learning, shared that responsibility with their students, and everybody won. There are good feelings all around. One of the accountability demands of the community was satisfied with the presentation of credible evidence of student success, and the new writing program was the reason for improved student achievement. Obviously, this story has a happy ending.

Success from the Student's Point of View

The day after the board meeting, I interviewed Emily about the evening's events. As you read, think about how our conversation centers on what really works for Emily.

"You did a nice job at the school board meeting last night, Emily," I started.

"Thanks," she replied. "What's most exciting for me is that, last year, I could never have done it."

"What's changed from last year?"

"I guess I'm more confident. I knew what had happened for me in English class and I wanted to tell them my story."

"You became a confident writer."

"Yeah, but that's not what I mean. Last night at the board meeting I was more than a good writer. I felt good talking about my writing and how I'd improved. It's like, I understand what had happened to me and I have a way to describe it."

"Let's talk about Emily the confident writer. What were you thinking last night when the board members were reacting to your initial writing sample—you know, the one that wasn't very good? Still confident?"

"Mom helped. She squeezed my hand and I remember she whispered in my ear, "You'll show 'em!" That helped me handle it. It's funny, I was listening to their comments to see if they knew anything about good writing. I wondered if they understood as much about it as I do—like, maybe they needed to take Ms. Weathersby's class."

"How did they do?" I asked, laughing.

"Pretty well, actually," Em replied. "They found some problems in my early work and described them pretty well. When I first started last fall, I wouldn't have been able to do that. I was a terrible writer."

"How do you know that, Em?"

"Now I understand where I was then, how little I could do. No organization. I didn't even know my own voice. No one had ever taken the time to show me the secrets. I'd never learned to analyze my writing. I wouldn't have known what to look for or how to describe it or how to change it. That's part of what Ms. W. taught us."

"How did she do that?"

"To begin with, she taught us to do what the board members did last night: analyze other people's writing. We looked at newspaper editorials, passages from books we were reading, letters friends had sent us. She wanted us to see what made those pieces work or not work. She would read a piece to us and then we'd brainstorm what made it good or bad. Pretty soon, we began to see patterns—things that worked or didn't work. She wanted us to begin to see and hear stuff as she read out loud."

"Like what?" I asked.

"Well, look, here's my early piece from the meeting last night. See, just read it!"

(Please read the Beginning of the Year Sample in Figure 2-3.)

Figure 2-3   **Beginning of the Year Writing Sample**

Computers are a thing of the future. They help us in thousands of ways. Computers are a help to our lives. They make things easier. They help us to keep track of information.

Computers are simple to use. Anyone can learn how. You do not have to be a computer expert to operate a computer. You just need to know a few basic things.

Computers can be robots that will change our lives. Robots are really computers! Robots do a lot of the work that humans used to do. This makes our lives much easier. Robots build cars and do many other tasks that humans used to do. When robots learn to do more, they will take over most of our work. This will free humans to do other kinds of things. You can also communicate on computers. It is much faster than mail! You can look up information, too. You can find information on anything at all on a computer.

Computers are changing the work and changing the way we work and communicate. In many ways, computers are changing our lives and making our lives better and easier.

Source: Personal writing by Nikki Spandel. Reprinted by permission.

"See, there are no grammar or usage mistakes. So it's 'correct' in that sense. But these short, choppy sentences just don't work. And it doesn't say anything or go anywhere. It's just a bunch of disconnected thoughts. It doesn't grab you and hold your attention. Then it just stops. It just ends. Now look at my second piece to see the difference."

(Please read the End of the Year Sample in Figure 2-4.)

Figure 2-4   **End of the Year Writing Sample**

So there I was, my face aglow with the reflection on my computer screen, trying to come up with the next line for my essay. Writing it was akin to Chinese water torture, as I could never seem to end it. It dragged on and on, a never-ending babble of stuff.

Suddenly, unexpectedly—I felt an ending coming on. I could wrap this thing up in four or five sentences, and this dreadful assignment would be over. I'd be free.

I had not saved yet, and decided I would do so now. I clasped the slick, white mouse in my hand, slid it over the mouse pad, and watched as the black arrow progressed toward the "File" menu. By accident, I clicked the mouse button just to the left of paragraph 66. I saw a flash and the next thing I knew, I was back to square one. I stared at the blank screen for a moment in disbelief. Where was my essay? My ten-billion-page masterpiece? Gone?! No—that couldn't be! Not after all the work I had done! Would a computer be that unforgiving? That unfeeling? Didn't it care about me at all?

I decided not to give up hope just yet. The secret was to remain calm. After all, my file had to be somewhere—right? That's what all the manuals say—"It's in there somewhere." I went back to the "File" menu, much more carefully this time. First, I tried a friendly sounding category called "Find File." No luck there; I hadn't given the file a name.

Ah, then I had a brainstorm. I could simply go up to "Undo." Yes, that would be my savior! A simple click of a button and my problem would be solved! I went to Undo, but it looked a bit fuzzy. Not a good sign. That means there is nothing to undo. Don't panic ... don't panic ...

I decided to try to exit the program, not really knowing what I would accomplish by this but feeling more than a little desperate. Next, I clicked on the icon that would allow me back in to word processing. A small sign appeared, telling me that my program was being used by another user. Another user? What's it talking about? I'm the only user, you idiot! Or at least I'm trying to be a user! Give me my paper back! Right now!

I clicked on the icon again and again—to no avail. Click ... click ... clickclickclickCLICKCLICKCLICK!!!! Without warning, a thin cloud of smoke began to rise from the back of the computer. I didn't know whether to laugh or cry. Sighing, I opened my desk drawer, and pulled out a tablet and pen. It was going to be a long day.

Source: Personal writing by Nikki Spandel. Reprinted by permission.

"In this one, I tried to tell about the feelings of frustration that happen when humans use machines. See, I think the voice in this piece comes from the feeling that 'We've all been there.' Everyone who works with computers has had this experience. A writer's tiny problem (not being able to find a good ending) turns into a major problem (losing the whole document). This idea makes the piece clear and organized. I think the reader can picture this poor, frustrated writer at her computer, wanting, trying to communicate in a human way—but finding that the computer is just as frustrated with her!"

"You sound just like you did last night at the board meeting."

"I'm always like this about my writing now. I know what works. Sentences are important. So is voice. So are organization and word choice—all that stuff. If you do it right, it works and you know it," she replied with a smile.

"What kinds of things did Ms. W. do in class that worked for you?"

"Well, like, when we were first getting started, Ms. Weathersby gave us a big stack of student papers she'd collected over the years—some good, some bad, and everything in between. Our assignment was to sort them into four stacks based on quality, from real good to real bad. When we were done, we compared who put what papers in which piles and then we talked about why. Sometimes, the discussions got pretty heated! Ms. W. wanted us to describe what we thought were the differences among the piles. Over time, we formed those differences into a set of rating scales that we used to analyze, evaluate, and improve our writing."

"Did you evaluate your own work or each other's?"

"Only our own to begin with. Ms. W. said she didn't want anyone being embarrassed. We all had a lot to learn. It was supposed to be private until we began to trust our own judgments. She kept saying, 'Trust me. You'll get better at this and then you can share.'"

"Did you ever move on to evaluating each other's work?"

"Yeah. After a while, we began to trust ourselves and each other. Then we were free to ask classmates for opinions. But Ms. W. said, no blanket judgments—no saying just, this is good or bad. And we were always supposed to be honest. If we couldn't see how to help someone improve a piece, we were supposed to say so."

"Were you able to see improvement in your writing along the way?" I wondered.

"Yeah, see, Ms. W. said that was the whole idea. I've still got my writing portfolio full of practice, see? It starts out pretty bad back in the fall and slowly gets pretty good toward spring. This is where the two pieces came from that the board read last night. I picked them. I talk about the changes in my writing in the self-reflections in here. My portfolio tells the whole story. Want to look through it?"

"I sure do. What do you think Ms. Weathersby did that was right, Emily?"

"Nobody had ever been so clear with me before about what it took to be really good at school stuff. It's like, there's no mystery—no need to psych her out. She said, 'I won't ever surprise you, trust me. I'll show you what I want and I don't want any excuses. But you've got to deliver good writing in this class. You don't deliver, you don't succeed.'

"Every so often, she would give us something she had written, so we could rate and provide her with feedback on her work. She listened to our comments and said it really helped her improve her writing. All of a sudden, we became her teachers! That was so cool!

"You know, she was the first teacher ever to tell me that it was okay not to be very good at something at first, like, when you're trying to do something new. But we couldn't stay there. We had to get a little better each time. If we didn't, it was our own fault. She didn't want us to give up on ourselves. If we kept improving, over time, we could learn to write well. I wish every teacher would do that. She would say, 'There's no shortage of success around here. You learn to write well, you get an A. My goal is to have everyone learn to write well and deserve an A.'"

"Thanks for filling in the details, Em."

"Thank you for asking!"

The Path to Assessment Balance and Quality

STUDENT
SUCCESS

Teacher
Competencies

Planning
for
Action

Required Skills
for Assessment
Balance and Quality

The Path to Assessment
Balance and Quality

Building the Vision

Laying the Foundation

The Building Blocks of Assessment Success

The Path to Assessment Balance and Quality

I n Part 2 we examined a vision of excellence in local assessment systems. The three main concepts of balance, quality, and student involvement form the core of our vision; should any of them be missing, schools run the risks of not meeting the information needs of key decision makers, misrepresenting student achievement due to poor-quality assessments, and missing out on proven student learning opportunities when the strategies of assessment *for* learning are not applied in the classroom.

As we discussed, leadership in assessment begins with such a guiding vision, centered on assessment as part of effective instruction—how it can promote student learning as well as measure it. School leaders will need to understand the necessity of quality assessment effectively used at every level, and be able to guide assessment practices in every school and classroom.

To turn your vision into reality, we encourage school leaders to consider seven essential assessment actions (introduced in Part 1). To ensure access to dependable evidence of achievement,

1. Balance the district's assessment system to meet all key user needs.

2. Refine achievement standards to reflect clear and appropriate expectations at all levels.

3. Ensure assessment quality in all contexts to support good decision making.

To ensure the effective use of that evidence,

4. Help learners become assessors by using assessment *for* learning strategies in the classroom.

5. Build communication systems to support and report student learning.

6. Motivate students with learning success

7. Provide the professional development needed to ensure a foundation of assessment literacy throughout the system.

Part 3 of this guide will help you to answer three questions:

Where are we going?

Answers to this question will define what it looks like when each of the Seven Actions has been implemented in your school or district. We'll examine some mistaken beliefs to abandon, look at the rationale for change in each Action and discuss the implications for student success.

Where are we now?

This question asks you to collect whatever evidence you may have that reflects the progress your school/district has made or is making in implementing each Action. Part 3 asks you to analyze the current status of your assessment system with respect to each action. Are you just starting? How far have you progressed? Have you already hit the target?

What can we do to close the gap?

The answers here are aimed at considerations of next steps that will help your school system get closer to the goal of assessment balance and quality.

Beginning Your School or District Self-Evaluation

In this section you begin an analysis that will result in a profile of where your school or district stands now relative to assessment balance, quality, and effective use. For each of the Seven Actions, we present a set of rating scales with performance continua related to that Action. The tables are intended to assist with individual reflection. When combined, these seven tables form a School/District Assessment System Self-Evaluation, which appears at the end of Part 3 in Activity 5 on pages 84–94 and on the accompanying CD-ROM. We suggest that the school or district leadership team conduct this self-evaluation as a group, *after* each team member has read about the Seven Actions and considered the rating scales for each.

Action 1: Balance Your Assessment System

This is the first of three Actions aimed at ensuring the dependability of evidence of student learning.

As defined in Part 2, balanced assessment systems meet the information needs of all relevant assessment users from the classroom to the boardroom. Different assessment users need access to different forms of assessment results at different times to do their jobs.

We have established that some instructional decisions are made once a year and require access to annual standardized test results. Some of these want to serve summative or accountability purposes: Are enough students succeeding at meeting standards? Others focus on program improvement or formative purposes: Which standards are students struggling to master and what can be done about it long term?

Other instructional decisions come up periodically, say, every few weeks and require information from more frequent standardized interim/benchmark assessments. Some serve formative purposes: Which standards are students struggling to master and what can be done about it right now? Others play a summative role: Do these results suggest that this program of instruction should be continued, improved, or changed in any way?

And finally, we have established that many instructional decisions are made moment to moment and day to day in the classroom. These require access to high-quality continuous classroom assessment results. Some are intended to support learning: What comes next in this student's learning? These are the formative applications. Others serve summative purposes: What report card grade should this student receive?

If the mission of schools is to raise the achievement of all learners and close gaps between those who meet and don't meet standards, then every local assessment system must be in balance. As stated earlier, if any of these levels of assessment fails to serve its intended purposes the other levels cannot pick up the slack. This leads directly to the self-study question for this Action: Is your assessment system in balance?

> *If the mission of schools is to raise the achievement of all learners and close gaps between those who meet and don't meet standards, then every local assessment system must be in balance.*

Is Your Assessment System in Balance?

Balanced assessment systems blend effective assessment use at the classroom level with interim/benchmark assessment and annual testing to serve both formative and summative purposes. This Action urges examination of current levels of balance and movement toward greater balance if needed. See Table 3-1 to help determine your current state of balance.

Table 3-1 **Action One: Balance the District's Assessment System to Meet All Key User Needs**

5 Implemented	4	3 Progressing	2	1 Getting Started
All faculty and staff are aware of differences in assessment purpose across classroom, interim/benchmark, and annual levels, and know how to use each to support and/or verify student learning; that is, to balance formative with summative assessment. We also understand what uses can and cannot be made with each level of assessment.		There is inconsistency among staff regarding assessment purpose, and some confusion about what is formative and what is summative. We are aware of the need for balance and have begun to plan for a balanced system.		There is little understanding of differences in purpose and assessment users, or appropriate uses of results across classroom, interim/benchmark, and annual levels.
A top assessment priority is to help students develop the capacity to assess their own learning and to use assessment results to help promote further learning.		Some faculty and staff recognize that students are important users of assessment information who make data-based instructional decisions that impact their own success, and have made some progress in helping them do so.		Students have not been viewed as key assessment users and there is little awareness of the benefits of bringing them into the assessment process, or knowledge of how to do so.
We have a comprehensive assessment system in place that defines a philosophy of assessment, states the roles assessment can play, and is meeting the information needs of all users. The plan coordinates state-, district-, and building-level tests, and supports administrators and teachers in bringing assessment balance to the district and its classrooms.		We know the need to do some systemwide planning around assessment and are in the process of developing an action plan to get there.		As yet, no such system has been conceived, designed, or developed. Most of our system is made up of large-scale, standardized testing from the state level.

Table 3-1 **Action One** *(continued)*

5 Implemented	4	3 Progressing	2	1 Getting Started
Policies at the district and school levels reflect the value placed on assessment balance and quality, and we have identified all of those policies that contribute to balanced and productive assessment, and have a systemic approach to the development and coordination of those policies.		We have some policies that support sound assessment practice but they are inconsistent across schools and/or at the district level. We don't always know yet what language needs to be used/replaced.		Our policies have not yet been examined for their role in supporting assessment balance and quality.
We have an information management system to collect, house, and deliver achievement information to users at classroom, interim/benchmark, and annual assessment levels.		We have an information management system but have not integrated its use across levels.		As yet no such system has been developed or purchased.
Our school board and community understand the concept and need for a balanced assessment system and are supportive of this priority.		We are currently educating our staff, policymakers, and community on the need to develop an assessment system to meet diverse information needs across levels.		Our policymakers and community are unaware of the need to think of assessment in this manner and view assessment mostly in the traditional role of measurement.
We have inventoried all assessments used in the district and have categorized them by purpose, standards/targets measured, time of year, etc. for the purpose of understanding the balance we have in our current assessment system.		We are in the process of identifying all of the various assessments used at the district and school level for the purpose of getting a clearer understanding of what is currently in our assessment system.		We do not have a comprehensive picture of what assessments are currently being given.

Deepening Your Understanding of Balanced Assessment Systems

The leaders of the Elmbrook School District in Brookfield, WI, were committed to creating a sound and balanced assessment system. The leaders knew that to develop such a system would take time and long-term commitment. To keep this vision at the forefront of decision making—when and how to do it—district leaders created a simple tabular representation (Table 3-2). Various levels of stakeholders had input in shaping the vision.

Table 3-2 presents what the three types of assessment measure and the Elmbrook School District's primary and secondary purposes for the assessments. The first column describes the assessments administered once a year, developed by national or state testing organizations. The second column represents the common assessments developed by teams of grade-level or content-area teachers in the school district. The third column represents the assessments developed or used by teachers in daily classroom instruction. With national and state testing, the primary purpose centers on accountability and program planning. With both district interim/benchmark and class-room assessments primary purposes center on informing students for decision making in learning and informing teachers for decision making in instruction. National and state secondary purposes center on improving curriculum, instructional delivery, and goal setting for individual students. Interim/benchmark assessment secondary pur-poses center on program accountability. Classroom assessment purposes are entirely primary.

Another beneficial step in understanding your assessment system's current status is to inventory all assessments being used and categorize them by purpose, standards/targets measured, time of year, and so on. Balance is desirable not only in assess-ment purpose but also in targets measured, assessment methods used, and time of year when measured. You may find that you currently underassess some targets and overassess others, or that you assess more at one time of the year than another. And you may discover that your school or district relies predominantly on one method of assessment, such as selected response tests. Doing so may either mismeasure learning targets not well suited to that method or ignore a whole section of the curriculum. Activities 3 and 4 help you perform your assessment inventory.

Table 3-2   **Elmbrook School District Document Showing Balance in Purpose**

Norm-referenced Assessment	Criterion-referenced Assessment	Criterion-referenced Assessment
National and State	**District**	**Classroom**
Standardized Administration	*Standardized Administration*	*Nonstandardized Administration*
ITBS (Grades 2, 6) CogATs (Grades 2, 3, 6, 8) WSAS (Grades 4, 8, 10) ACT High School SAT High School State Reading Test (Grade 3)	K–2 Literacy Benchmark Assessment 3–5 Benchmark Assessment 6–8 Benchmark Assessment 9–12 Benchmark Assessment	Ongoing Assessment • paper/pencil • personal communication • observation • performance
Assess		
Reading, Writing, Language, Math, Science, Social Studies, Study Skills	All Curricular Areas (in development)	All Curricular Areas
Primary Purposes for Data		
• Reporting/sharing progress with students, parents, and community • Program accountability and comparisons of performance • Improving curriculum and instructional delivery of programs • Reporting to federal and state agencies	• Reporting/sharing progress with students and parents • Improving curriculum and instructional delivery for individual students • Setting learning goals for/with individual students	• Reporting/sharing progress with students and parents • Improving curriculum and instructional delivery for individual students • Setting learning goals for/with individual students
Secondary Purposes for Data		
• Improving curriculum and instructional delivery for individual students • Setting goals for/with individual students	• Program accountability	

Source: Copyright © 1994 School District of Elmbrook, Brookfield, WI. Adapted with permission.

Thinking About Assessment
Activity 3: Formative or Summative?

Purpose:

Balanced systems blend assessments across multiple levels for both summative and formative purposes. Although any assessment can be used in both ways, some are more suited for one use or the other, and in fact are designed for that primary use. In this activity participants classify each assessment type listed as either formative or summative.

Activity 3 is a precursor to Activity 4, Conducting an Assessment Audit. That activity asks teams to build an inventory of assessments being conducted in their school or district and analyze it on a number of levels. Understanding and agreeing on what is and is not formative or summative as practiced in this activity will help you conduct your audit.

Time:

20–30 minutes

Materials Needed:

Copies for each participant of Table 3-3, "Formative or Summative?" as shown in this book (also found on the accompanying CD-ROM), with the right column blank

Suggested Room Setup:

No special room arrangements needed

Directions:

- Make sure every participant is viewing a copy of Table 3-3. Give everyone a few minutes to read the column headings across the top of the table and the row headings in the lefthand column. Notice that the righthand column of the table headed "Is the use formative or summative?" is left blank.

- After everyone has reviewed the table, discuss each row to determine whether its use is formative or summative. Attempt to reach consensus on each example. If there is disagreement, team members should explain their classification rationale by answering the question(s), "What is formative/summative about that use?" Remember that many assessments can pull double duty, but for this activity the focus is on the use as given. You may find that some uses you classify as formative may also extend into assessment *for* learning where students are also involved in improving learning.

- When you have completed your discussions, refer to the authors' completed table (this version appears on the accompanying CD-ROM only). Discuss any differences of opinion.

Table 3-3 **Formative or Summative?**

Type of assessment	What is the purpose?	Who will use the information?	How will it be used?	Is the use formative or summative?
State test	Measure level of achievement on state content standards	State	Determine AYP	
		District, Teacher Teams	Determine program effectiveness	
	Identify percentage of students meeting performance standards on state content standards	State	Comparison of schools/districts	
		District, Teacher Teams	Develop programs/interventions for groups or individuals	
District benchmark, interim, or common assessment	Measure level of achievement toward state content standards	District, Teacher Teams	Determine program effectiveness	
		District, Teacher Teams	Identify program needs	
	Identify students needing additional help	District, Teacher Teams, Teachers	Plan interventions for groups or individuals	
Classroom assessment	Measure level of achievement on learning targets taught	Teachers	Determine report card grade	
	Diagnose student strengths and areas needing reteaching	Teacher Teams, Teachers	Revise teaching plans for next year/semester	
			Plan further instruction/differentiate instruction for these students	
		Teachers, Students	Provide feedback to students	
	Understand strengths and areas needing work	Students	Self-assess, set goals for further study/work	

Source: Adapted from *Seven Strategies of Assessment for Learning* (p. 8), by J. Chappuis, 2009, Portland, OR: Educational Testing Service. Adapted by permission.

Thinking About Assessment
Activity 4: Conducting an Assessment Audit

Purpose:

This activity helps schools and districts map the "big picture" of the tests administered and helps inform school leaders as to what assessments outside the classroom are currently at work in the school/district. The assessment audit acts as an inventory, assisting leaders by providing information on what learning expectations assessments measure, when assessments are given, how much time each one takes, and each assessment's purpose. Administrators then use it to manage their local assessment system, analyze its contents, and find testing gaps and redundancies relative to academic standards (Office of Superintendent of Public Instruction, 1996 [hereafter referred to as OSPI]).

The information collected through the audit is also useful when merging a local with a state assessment system and ensuring that they work together and don't overlap. Assessment audit results also are valuable when communicating with parents about standardized test administration and results. Once each test's audit data (time, purpose, standards assessed, methods used, scoring procedures, etc.) are catalogued, schools can use the information to create a letter to parents to provide them pertinent assessment information.

The activity has three parts. Each part contains a blank table grid for you to fill out with your relevant information. (Full-page copies of these grids, suitable for writing in, appear on the accompanying CD-ROM.) You can create other grids suitable to your local program, to help paint a picture of the total testing program in your school or district. Note that this activity involves gathering information from a variety of sources.

Time:

Variable; multiple sessions over the course of a day or longer

Materials Needed:

School calendars or other documents that detail or list assessments being administered to students

Suggested Room Setup:

No special room arrangements needed

PART 1: A Model for Identifying Gaps in Your Assessment Plan

Directions:

1. Once you have gathered your assessment documentation, categorize the details according to the column headings.

2. Examine the data to determine if the assessments are meeting the needs of all users.

3. Determine if there are redundancies in measurement of the content standards.

4. Determine the overall balance of standards/targets measured; times of year for the administration.

Name/form of each standard-ized test or other assessment administered *(list by content area or test battery separately)*	Grade level(s) tested	Time of year given	Total testing time	Specific state standards assessed by this instrument	Assessment method(s) used	Connection to the district curriculum	Intended uses and users of test results	Communication plans

PART 2: Record of Required State, District, and School Assessments*

The prior organizer helped you to focus on the overall picture of assessment within your system. The following organizer assists you in focusing on the use of assessments across grade levels and content areas.

Directions:

1. Using the same assessment documents as for Part 1 of this activity, categorize the assessments by both the grade level administered and the content area being measured. Also, determine what level of the system requires their administration.

2. Determine if there is balance in what is being measured across grade levels and content areas. Are some grade levels or content areas overassessed or underassessed? Is there balance in meeting informational needs—who is requiring the information and when?

---

*Developed with Dr. Linda Elman, Central Kitsap School District, WA.

	Math	Language	Reading	Science	Social Studies	Other	Total State Required	Total District Required	Total School Required	Total
Grade 2										
Grade 3										
Grade 4										
Grade 5										

PART 3: Assessments in Math (or other content area)*

This organizer allows you to narrow your analysis and determine balance across any single given content area. This example uses math, but any content area could be the focus.

Directions:

1. Categorize the data according to the column headings.

2. Analyze the data for balance in purpose, users, and grade levels tested.

3. Do the assessments acknowledge all of the users of the assessment information?

4. Does the assessment information meet all users' needs?

5. Are some grade levels underassessed? Overassessed?

Test Name	Test Uses: Purpose	Test Users	School Level	District Level	Classroom Level	Methods Used	Time Needed	K	1	2	3	4	5	6	7	8	9	10	11	12

---

* Adapted from Office of Superintendent of Public Instruction, 1996.

Action 2: Refine Achievement Standards

This is the second of three Actions aimed at ensuring the quality of the evidence used to inform instructional decisions.

Clear and appropriate achievement standards are fundamental to assessments at all levels because they define what is to be assessed. We cannot dependably assess targets that are not completely clear and defined. The good news is that state and local education agencies have spent the past two decades defining academic achievement standards. In addition, professional associations of teachers and school leaders have made important contributions to the establishment of clear targets. And, at the time of this writing, the Council of Chief State School Officers in partnership with the National Governors Association is working to identify core national achievement standards in mathematics, reading, and writing. Our collective vision of the meaning of academic success continues to come into sharper focus.

But there may still be work to do at the district level. It is possible that some state standards do not represent a sufficient definition of academic success in and of themselves. If they do not guide daily instruction at the classroom level, more refinement will be needed.

When this is the case, district and school leaders can refine state or national standards by identifying essential expectations and adding clarity where needed. In addition, standards should be properly sequenced in each subject over time within and across grade levels in a way that supports classroom instruction and student learning. Further, each standard needs to be deconstructed into the scaffolding students will ascend during their learning. It is this process that identifies what the standard looks like as targets of daily instruction for the classroom teacher. This allows classroom assessments to reflect and measure the learning targets on the rungs of the ascent, not achievement of the standards themselves. And finally, those classroom-level (scaffolding) learning targets must be transformed into student-friendly versions that teachers can share with their students (and parents) from the very beginning of the learning.

Responsibility for these improvements when needed lies with states and with local school districts. This is not work that can or should be done teacher by teacher. Qualified state and local teams or subcommittees can refine standards into grade-level or subject area indicators, and prepare student- and even family-friendly versions of achievement expectations.

What Is the Current State of Your Achievement Standards?

Achievement standards are fundamental to any assessment system. That is, clear learning targets are needed to underpin classroom, interim/benchmark, and annual assessments. This Action calls for developing local achievement expectations as a foundation for balanced assessment. Table 3-4 shows the stages in this development.

Table 3-4 **Action Two: Refine Achievement Standards to Reflect Clear and Appropriate Expectations at All Levels**

5 Implemented	4	3 Progressing	2	1 Getting Started
We continue to refine our local achievement standards, have aligned them with state standards, and have identified our highest-priority learning outcomes.		We are aware of the need to develop clear local academic standards aligned to state standards and are in the process of doing so. What is in place is not yet used consistently across classrooms.		Local learning expectations are not in place.
Assessment results for all uses are always linked back to the local content standards.		We can link some assessments back to our written curriculum, but don't always know how or why we should do that.		We use the results as they are delivered to us and have yet to take the extra step of consistently matching results to the written curriculum.
We have deconstructed our standards into knowledge, reasoning, performance skills, and product development learning targets at each grade level for each subject.		We are in the process of deconstructing each of our standards into the scaffolding of grade-level curricula.		The deconstruction process has not been initiated.
We have transformed the grade- and course-level learning targets that guide classroom assessment and instruction into student- and family-friendly versions.		Some of that work has been accomplished but we have not completed it for all grade levels and courses or it is not adequately communicated to parents and/or students.		We have yet to begin this process.

Table 3-4 **Action Two** (continued)

5 Implemented	4	3 Progressing	2	1 Getting Started
We have verified that each teacher in each classroom is master of the content standards that their students are expected to master. We provide professional support in content areas to teachers when needed.		We have identified contexts in which professional development is needed to ensure teacher competence in terms of our standards and that learning is underway.		There has been no investigation of teacher preparedness in their own content area(s).
All teachers in the district have received adequate training and ongoing support in developing their understanding of the written curricular documents. Teachers are given time to collaboratively plan lessons aimed at accomplishing grade-level/subject expectations.		We share curricular documents with our teachers. If there are questions about the new curriculum we address them, and provide some training at the beginning of the year in the understanding and use of those documents.		The curricular documents are available on request or are given to teachers when the documents have undergone revisions.
A curriculum implementation plan is in place to ensure consistency in achievement expectations across classrooms. Teachers are held accountable for teaching the written curriculum.		We recognize a need for a curriculum implementation plan to ensure the written curriculum is the taught curriculum, and have taken some steps to ensure that.		We have not ensured that there is consistency in achievement expectations across teachers. What is taught in each classroom in the same subject/grade level can differ widely.
Model/sample lessons and assessments, linked to the content standards, are available and used for professional development.		This is true for some subjects and grade levels.		We do not have this in our school/district.

Deepening Your Understanding of Refined Standards

Develop or Refine Academic Standards

Clear, relevant, rigorous achievement standards are the district's declaration of accountability in what students must know and be able to do. If this work has not yet been done or is incomplete, district leaders will need to organize representatives from all content areas and across all grade levels to complete the task. Those local standards should be all of the following:

Clear	Clearly stated and understandable by the teachers and students within the district as well as by members of the community the district serves
Aligned	Aligned with state standards for accountability purposes
Essential	Reflect what is truly important to learn; what is the heart of the discipline; what will have leverage in mastering the next level of learning; what will prepare students not only to do well today but five, ten, twenty years down the road
Realistic	Achievable by students; that is, the time, the conditions, and the materials are available for the students to reach the targets
Measurable	What students have to know or do is measurable and can be assessed accurately; i.e., the outcomes in the standard statement are expressed in measurable terms
Developmental	The local standards unfold over time within and across grade levels consistent with the way learning happens; gaps and redundancies are avoided

When bringing teachers and administrators together to refine achievement standards, an important place to begin is with national curricular organizations such as the CCSSO/NGA Core Standards, National Council of Teachers of Mathematics, the International Reading Association, or the National Council of Teachers of English. These organizations have identified what they consider essential learning standards in their subject and they can provide the starting point for determining local curriculum.

We would also recommend that the committee begin the identification process with a "design down" model. Start with what students must know and be able to do at the end of their schooling; that is, at graduation. Then identify what they must know and be able to do at the end of eleventh grade, then tenth grade, then ninth grade, and so on. Keeping the end in mind will not only make identification easier, it will greatly eliminate gaps and redundancies. Also, having everyone on the committee hear what learning looks like at the end not only will help them identify appropriate grade-level standards, but also will focus on how important each teacher's job is in helping students learn in a manner consistent with the way learning progresses in the mastery of those standards.

Focusing on priority standards will result in a manageable list of expectations that teachers teach to and assess. Here is an example: A group of world language teachers identified their priority standards. At the end of twelfth grade students will be able to do the following:

- Interpret the spoken words of the target language.

- Communicate orally and fluently with others in the target language.

- Read for comprehension in the target language and for a variety of purposes.

- Write clearly and effectively for different purposes and different audiences.

- Compare and contrast the cultures of the target language with their own culture.

Deconstruct Standards

Once essential or priority standards are identified, small content-area committees will have another important function: deconstructing them into the everyday learning targets that are the foundation for teachers' daily lessons. The journey to mastering priority standards entails foundations of knowledge, reasoning, performance skills, or product development capabilities students must acquire along the way, and any curriculum can be classified using these four types of learning targets.

Thus, the world language teachers in our example concentrated on their five priority standards and further defined them. They indicated what the standards looked like at the end of each course and grade level, asking, for example, What does "Communicate orally with others" look like at the end of Level V, Level IV, Level III, Level II, Level I, and at the end of elementary school? They determined that at the end of Level V "Communicate orally with others" is the ability to hold extended conversations on various topics with different audiences using a variety of vocabulary and levels of syntax. At the end of Level I this standard is the ability to converse on familiar topics such as family and friends using simple sentences and phrases with basic vocabulary and in the present or future tense.

Table 3-5 provides another example of what can be done to refine standards, in this case to make them more easily and accurately assessable at the classroom level. (We'll provide more information about assessing accurately in Action 3.) In this case a writing standard has been deconstructed into the knowledge, reasoning, skill, and product targets that underpin the standard. These are the things students must know or be able to do at a particular grade level to show mastery of the standard. This example shows the same standard deconstructed and then classified by learning target for Grade 1 and for Grade 7.

Table 3-5 **Refining Curriculum: Classifying Targets**

Standard/Benchmark:

Produce writing to communicate with different audiences for a variety of purposes.

Type: ☑ Product ☐ Skill ☐ Reasoning ☐ Knowledge

What are the knowledge, reasoning, skill, or product targets underpinning the standard or benchmark?

Learning Targets: Grade 1

Product Targets	Skill Targets	Reasoning Targets	Knowledge Targets
Write sentences with varied beginnings	Hold a pencil correctly Print letters correctly according to DN methods Space words Use lines and margins correctly Stretch out sounds in words to create a temporary spelling of a word	Distinguish the uses or meanings of a variety of words (word choice)	Know what a sentence is Understand concept of word choice

Learning Targets: Grade 7

Product Targets	Skill Targets	Reasoning Targets	Knowledge Targets
Write a personal narrative on an event that made an impact on one's life	Write well so others can read handwriting Do word processing such as touch typing, spell checking, and using various formatting tools	Determine audience and purpose for writing Select ideas that are interesting to the author and audience Organize words, sentences, and paragraphs to make the ideas clear and the transitions smooth Distinguish among and select words and figures of speech that convey the author's thoughts and emotions to the reader Determine whether sentences flow and have variety Determine whether the layout is appropriate and the spelling, punctuation, and grammar are accurate	Describe the elements of a narrative piece of writing Identify the rules of capitalization, spelling, punctuation Identify complete sentences Identify important events and know what makes them important Identify logical sequence of events Identify beginning, middle, and end of a narrative Know strategies for drafting, revising, and editing one's own work

Student- and Family-friendly Learning Targets

The same team(s) developing or refining the academic standards and deconstructing the standards can also write those targets in student-friendly or parent-friendly language. (See Chapter 3 of *Classroom Assessment* for *Student Learning* [Stiggins et al., 2006] for in-depth discussion of writing student-friendly versions of learning targets.) This process will unify the language being used with students across all teachers and classrooms. Having a common curriculum language will benefit students, teachers, parents, and whoever else has a need to know, work with, and communicate about the targets.

Putting "family-friendly" targets on your district's or school's website will also help parents know what their students must master in their learning. It will make the classroom transparent to the parents and to the community as well. You will publicly declare your accountability in student learning. For example, Dana Broehl, a foreign language teacher in the Kettle Moraine School District in Wales, WI, keeps her website (http://www.kmsd.edu/webpages/dbroehl/) up to date, informing her students and others of the current unit learning targets. She has her priority and WebGrader standards on the site as well.

Teacher Mastery of Student Standards and Learning Targets

Districts and schools establish their academic expectations for students by developing a K–12 curriculum aligned with national and state standards. For students to succeed in meeting these standards, their teachers must be masters of the achievement targets their students are expected to hit, meaning that they must have command of the content knowledge in the subjects they are assigned to teach. If a teacher does not have such command, student learning will suffer at that time and in the future because those students will not have mastered prerequisites for the learning that follows.

Fixing such gaps in professional preparedness may require content-area professional development for some teachers, or may necessitate assigning mentors who will assist these teachers in developing subject-matter knowledge and skills. For example, if willing to help, the high school physics teacher is a treasure trove of knowledge for the elementary teacher who may be teaching motion and energy.

Special attention should be given to new teachers, many of whom may need specialized content training to better understand the standards, learning targets, and sample lessons, and the time to plan lessons aligned to the curriculum.

Creating a Curriculum Used by All Educators in the District

Once you have established a curriculum of standards and classroom-level learning targets, your next challenge is to make sure that the curriculum is not shelved on the back bookcase. Developing a sufficiently detailed and balanced curriculum may not be enough. The written curriculum also must be the taught curriculum—teachers should actively use it as their guide for lesson development, delivery, and assessment. It is essential that schools and districts provide teachers the time to work together to learn the curriculum, plan lessons and assessments, and continue their own learning in the academic disciplines they teach (Schmoker, 2002).

Action 3: Ensure Assessment Quality

This is the third of three Actions aimed at ensuring the quality of the evidence generated from student assessments.

It is not uncommon for communities to believe that the assessments used in their schools are of high quality and are therefore accurately portraying their children's achievement. Community members might be surprised to learn that many educators are, in fact, often unsure of assessment quality and have had little training in either assessment accuracy or the effective use of assessment results to promote student success. Many preservice programs continue to neglect this facet of professional preparation of teachers and school leaders, and inservice opportunities remain scarce. As a result, through no fault of their own, many educators lack the background needed to evaluate and ensure the quality of local assessments—classroom, common, or interim/benchmark.

Schools and teachers can accommodate differences in the needs of students only if they have dependable day-to-day evidence of their students' current levels of achievement. This Action calls for evaluating and verifying assessment quality.

Can You Ensure Assessment Quality?

Because a variety of decisions are made based on assessment results, all assessments at classroom, interim/benchmark, and annual levels of use must yield dependable information about student achievement. This Action urges the evaluation of current assessments to verify quality. Table 3-6 can help guide your evaluation of quality.

Table 3-6   **Action Three: Ensure Assessment Quality in All Contexts to Support Good Decision Making**

5 Implemented	4	3 Progressing	2	1 Getting Started
We have adopted and can apply the criteria by which we should judge the quality of our assessments, both *of* and *for* learning.		We have standards for assessment quality, and some district staff have the capability to evaluate for quality, but it is not a consistent condition in the district.		No such criteria have been identified; no quality control framework exists for us at any level.
There is general understanding that quality assessments form the foundation for accurate report card grades and for decisions made about students that rely on assessment data.		We subscribe to the use of multiple measures but haven't ensured that all data sources yield dependable results.		We've not considered this as a priority for our time/resources.
At the classroom level, teachers understand the importance of selecting the appropriate assessment method match to the type(s) of learning target to be assessed in order to help ensure quality results.		Teachers understand the need to vary assessment methods but may not apply strict quality criteria when doing so.		Teachers do not see the link between assessment quality and the assessment method used.
We have conducted a local evaluation of the quality of all of our assessments, including interim/benchmark and common assessments, if used.		We are aware of the need to conduct such an evaluation and are planning to conduct it.		There is no awareness of the need for or plans to conduct such an evaluation.

Deepening Your Understanding of Assessment Quality

Keys to Quality Assessment

Accurate and effective classroom assessments are built on a foundation that includes the following five key characteristics:

- Be designed to serve the specific information needs of intended users (clear purpose)

- Arise from clearly articulated and appropriate achievement targets (clear targets)

- Accurately reflect student achievement (quality assessment design)

- Yield results that are effectively communicated to their intended users (effective communication)

- When appropriate during learning, involve students in classroom assessment, record keeping, and communication (student involvement)

These keys were illustrated graphically in Part 2, Figure 2-1. This model is built around the need to (1) assess accurately and (2) use assessment to benefit students, not merely to grade and sort them.

A summary of key quality control criteria follows. For in-depth treatment of assessment quality for the purpose of transferring the knowledge to classroom practice, readers may refer to *Classroom Assessment* for *Student Learning* (Stiggins et al., 2006).

Whether functioning at classroom, interim/benchmark, or annual testing levels, sometimes assessment is to support learning, other times to verify or certify learning. Because of that, we have differentiated between assessments *for* learning and assessments *of* learning. Both are important, but they are different. With respect to assessment quality, then, developers cannot build an assessment that will work well within any particular context unless and until they know who will use the results and how. So, assessment development and use must start with a clear purpose. We addressed this previously under Action 1.

In addition to beginning with a purpose in mind, teachers, or others developing assessments, must also have a clear sense of the achievement expectations they wish students to master. Obviously, these achievement expectations are what they will be assessing. This was the focus of Action 2.

This leads us to the specific focus of this Action—the quality of the assessment itself. Assessments can produce accurate or inaccurate information about student achievement. They can correctly represent or misrepresent learning. The goal is accurate assessment, always.

The previous two keys to assessment quality, clear purpose and clear targets, lay a foundation of accuracy. An assessment devised without clear purpose or focus is extremely unlikely to produce accurate information. Accuracy also requires that developers pay close attention to three design features:

First, they must select a proper assessment method for each context. Each of the four assessment methods (selected response, written response, performance assessment, and personal communication) has unique strengths and limitations, and works well in some contexts but not in others. Assessment methods are not interchangeable.

The task always is to choose a proper method given the target(s) to be assessed—the quality of any assessment hinges on this. Table 3-7 matches achievement targets and assessment methods, noting which combinations make good matches and which do not.

Once assessors have chosen appropriate methods, they must develop quality assessment exercises (test questions, extended written response questions, or performance tasks) and scoring plans such as checklist, rubrics, points awarded for features, and so on. It means including enough items or exercises to lead to confident conclusions about student achievement without having to gather more evidence than the context requires.

Table 3-7 **Matching Assessment Methods to Learning Targets**

Target to be Assessed	Assessment Method			
	Selected Response/ Fill-In: Multiple-choice, True/False, Matching, Fill-In	**Written Response**	**Performance Assessment**	**Personal Communication**
Knowledge	*Good*—can assess isolated elements of knowledge and some relationships among them	*Strong*—can assess elements of knowledge and relationships among them	*Partial*—can assess elements of knowledge and relationships among them in the context of certain tasks	*Strong*—can assess elements of knowledge and relationships among them
Reasoning	*Good*—can assess many, but not all, reasoning targets	*Strong*—can assess all reasoning targets	*Good*—can assess reasoning targets in the context of certain tasks	*Strong*—can assess all reasoning targets
Performance Skill	*Poor*—cannot assess skill level; can only assess prerequisite knowledge and reasoning targets		*Strong*—can observe and assess skills as they are being performed	*Partial*—strong match for some oral communication proficiencies; not a good match otherwise
Product	*Poor*—cannot assess skill level; can only assess prerequisite knowledge and reasoning targets	*Partial*—strong match for some written learning targets; not a good match otherwise	*Strong*—can directly assess the attributes of quality products	*Poor*—cannot assess the quality of the product; can only assess prerequisite knowledge and reasoning targets

Source: Adapted from *An Introduction to Student-Involved Assessment FOR Learning*, 5th ed. (p. 81), by Rick Stiggins, 2008, Upper Saddle River, NJ: Pearson Education. Adapted by permission.

Finally, every assessment situation brings with it its own list of things that can go wrong and that can distort results—these represent sources of bias. For instance, a score on any assessment can misrepresent a student's real achievement if the test questions are poorly written, the directions are misleading, the student suffers from extreme test anxiety, or subjective scoring procedures for extended response or performance assessments are conducted carelessly. It is every assessor's responsibility to anticipate what can go wrong in various assessment contexts and prevent those problems when possible.

To ensure accuracy, over and above starting with clear targets and information needs, all involved in any assessment must do the following:

- Rely on proper assessment methods for each particular context.
- Build the assessment with high-quality items and/or tasks.
- Sample student achievement appropriately.
- Rely only on quality exercises and scoring procedures to avoid potential sources of bias.

Table 3-8 will assist teachers and administrators in connecting the keys to quality to their own assessment context. The left column identifies each key, the column to the right translates the key into specific teacher classroom assessment competencies.

Action 4: Help Learners Become Assessors by Using Assessment *for* Learning Strategies in the Classroom

The next three Actions form the foundation of the overarching concept of assessment *for* learning.

Action 4 advocates use of classroom assessment activities that acknowledge (1) that students are key instructional decision makers too, and (2) that their interpretation of their assessment results can lead them either to confidence and engagement or to a sense that their effort to learn is futile. The principles of assessment *for* learning engage students in self-assessment in ways that promote hope, keeping them believing that success is within reach if they keep trying.

As stated, the possibility exists that struggling learners will interpret low scores as evidence that their failure is inevitable. This can cause them to give up. But the good news is that when students play a role in their own assessment, teachers can help them turn a feeling of failure around 180 degrees.

The question is, Can educators help students maintain confidence in themselves so they will want to continue trying? The answer is, Yes they can. Doing so calls for

Table 3-8 **Indicators of Sound Classroom Assessment Practice***

1. Why Assess? Assessment Processes and Results Serve Clear and Appropriate Purposes	a. Teachers understand who and what the users and uses of classroom assessment information are and know their information needs. b. Teachers understand the relationship between assessment and student motivation and craft assessment experiences to maximize motivation. c. Teachers use classroom assessment processes and results formatively (assessment *for* learning). d. Teachers use classroom assessment results summatively (assessment *of* learning) to inform someone beyond the classroom about students' achievement as of a particular point in time. e. Teachers have a comprehensive plan over time for integrating assessment *for* and *of* learning in the classroom.
2. Assess What? Assessments Reflect Clear and Valued Student Learning Targets	a. Teachers have clear learning targets for students; they know how to turn broad statements of content standards into classroom-level targets. b. Teachers understand the various types of learning targets they hold for students. c. Teachers select learning targets focused on the most important things students need to know and be able to do. d. Teachers have a comprehensive plan over time for assessing learning targets.
3. Assess How? Learning Targets Are Translated into Assessments That Yield Accurate Results	a. Teachers understand what the various assessment methods are. b. Teachers choose assessment methods that match intended learning targets. c. Teachers design assessments that serve intended purposes. d. Teachers sample learning appropriately in their assessments. e. Teachers write assessment questions of all types well. f. Teachers avoid sources of bias that distort results.
4. Communicate How? Assessment Results Are Managed Well and Communicated Effectively	a. Teachers record assessment information accurately, keep it confidential, and appropriately combine and summarize it for reporting (including grades). Such summary accurately reflects current level of student learning. b. Teachers select the best reporting option (grades, narratives, portfolios, conferences) for each context (learning targets and users). c. Teachers interpret and use standardized test results correctly. d. Teachers effectively communicate assessment results to students. e. Teachers effectively communicate assessment results to a variety of audiences outside the classroom, including parents, colleagues, and other stakeholders.
5. Involve Students How? Students Are Involved in Their Own Assessment	a. Teachers make learning targets clear to students. b. Teachers involve students in assessing, tracking, and setting goals for their own learning. c. Teachers involve students in communicating about their own learning.

*Sound classroom assessment practice = Skill in gathering accurate information + effective use of information and procedures

Source: Reprinted from *Classroom Assessment* for *Student Learning: Doing It Right—Using It Well* (p. 27), by R. J. Stiggins, J. Arter, J. Chappuis, & S. Chappuis, 2006, Portland, OR: Assessment Training Institute. Copyright © 2006, 2004 by Educational Testing Service. Reprinted by permission.

the consistent application of classroom assessment *for* learning practices. These practices ask teachers to help students understand what good work looks like from the very beginning of learning, help students learn to self-assess by comparing their work to that standard of excellence to identify differences, and help students learn how to close the gap between the two (Sadler, 1989, as developed in Chappuis, 2009). To reiterate, when these are used routinely in classrooms, the result can be profound achievement gains for all students, with the largest gains coming for low achievers.

Are Your Learners Involved in Their Own Assessment?

By involving students in their own assessment during learning, teachers can maximize student confidence, motivation, and achievement. This Action urges that teachers involve them in all aspects of classroom assessment, understanding them as users of results just as they do themselves and others. Table 3-9 describes the levels of a school or district's implementation of student involvement in assessment.

Table 3-9 **Action Four: Help Learners Become Assessors by Using Assessment *for* Learning Strategies in the Classroom**

5 Implemented	4	3 Progressing	2	1 Getting Started
Faculty, staff, policymakers, and community members all understand and embrace the idea of assessment *for* learning—i.e., student-involved assessment to promote learning.		We are in the process of building local awareness of and belief in this set of ideas. Formative assessment is visible, but not as assessment *for* learning.		As yet, there is no awareness of the value of this concept or set of classroom practices.
Teachers use assessment information to focus instruction day to day in the classroom and communicate learning expectations to students in language they can understand.		Our primary use of formative assessment is at the interim or common assessment level, not exactly day-to-day at the classroom level. Some teachers know how to translate learning targets into student-friendly language, but many do not.		This has not been a focus or priority for us to date.
Teachers design assessments to help students self-assess and to help them use assessment results as feedback to set goals.		Some teachers administer assessments as practice; others need training to help them make that transition.		We don't involve students in the assessment process in these ways.

Deepening Your Understanding of Assessment *for* Learning Strategies in the Classroom

Increased Student Involvement

If students are to be active users of assessment results and involved in the assessment process, what does that look like? What do students need to be productive users of assessment information?

Sadler (1989) answers as follows: "The indispensable conditions for improvement are that the *student* comes to hold a concept of quality roughly similar to that held by the teacher, is able to monitor continuously the quality of what is being produced *during the act of production itself*, and has a repertoire of alternative moves or strategies from which to draw at any given point" (p. 121, emphasis in original).

Atkin, Black, and Coffey (2001) translate Sadler's conditions into three questions to define students' information needs met by effective formative assessment. Chappuis (2009) paraphrases these questions:

- Where am I going?
- Where am I now?
- How can I close the gap?

She then offers seven classroom strategies teachers may apply to involve students directly in the formative assessment process. We restate these strategies in the following pages, and amplify them to describe the lessons classroom teachers can learn through professional development that will best help them use assessment *for* learning with students.

Where Am I Going?

Strategy 1: Provide Students with a Clear and Understandable Vision of the Learning Target.

Motivation and achievement both increase when instruction is guided by clearly defined targets. Activities that help students answer the question, "What's the learning?" set the stage for all further formative assessment actions.

Share with your students the learning target(s), objective(s), or goal(s) in advance of teaching the lesson, giving the assignment, or doing the activity. Write targets in student-friendly language, and check to make sure they understand what the target means. Connect daily activities with these targets by asking, "Why are we doing this activity?" and "What are we learning?" Also, ask students what they think constitutes quality in a product or performance learning target and then show how their thoughts match with the scoring guide or rubric you will use to define quality. Provide students with scoring guides written in student-friendly language or develop scoring criteria with them.

Strategy 2: Use Examples and Models of Strong and Weak Work.

Carefully chosen examples and nonexamples can create and refine students' understanding of the learning goal by helping students answer the questions, "What defines quality work?" and "What are some problems to avoid?"

Use models of strong and weak work—anonymous student work, work from life beyond school, and your own work. Begin with work that demonstrates strengths and weaknesses related to problems students commonly experience, especially the problems that most concern you. Students analyze these anonymous samples for quality and then justify their judgments. When you engage students in analyzing examples or models, they will be developing a vision of what the product or performance looks like when it's done well.

You also can model creating a product or performance, showing students the true beginnings, the problems they may run into, and how to think through decisions along the way. Students will see what it looks like working through both the easy and the hard parts. It is part of the learning.

Where Am I Now?

Strategy 3: Offer Regular Descriptive Feedback.

Effective feedback shows students where they are on their path to attaining the intended learning. It answers for students the questions, "What are my strengths?"; "What do I need to work on?"; and "Where did I go wrong and what can I do about it?"

Offer descriptive feedback instead of grades on work that is for practice. This feedback should reflect student strengths and areas for improvement with respect to the specific learning target(s) they are trying to hit in a given assignment. Feedback is most effective when it identifies what students are doing right, as well as what they need to work on next. What did learners accomplish? What are the next steps? All learners, especially struggling ones, need to know that they did something right, and your job is to find it and label it for them before launching into what they need to improve.

Learners don't need to know everything that needs correcting, all at once. Narrow your comments to the specific knowledge and skills emphasized in the current assignment and pay attention to how much feedback learners can act on at one time. Students will not be harmed if you don't point out all of their problems. Identify as many issues as students can successfully act on at one time, independently, and then figure out what to teach next based on the other problems in their work.

Providing students with descriptive feedback is a crucial part of increasing achievement. Feedback helps students answer the question, "Where am I now?" with respect to "Where do I need to be?" You are also modeling the kind of thinking you want your students to engage in when they self-assess.

Strategy 4: Teach Students to Self-assess and Set Goals.

The information provided in effective feedback models the kind of thinking you want students to be able to do about their own work. Strategy 4 teaches them to identify their strengths and weaknesses and to set goals for further learning. It helps them answer the questions, "What am I good at?"; "What do I need to work on?"; and "What should I do next?"

Providing students with descriptive feedback is a crucial part of increasing achievement.

Self-assessment is a necessary part of learning, not an add-on if you have the time or the "right" students. Struggling students are as much the right students as any others. Studies Black and Wiliam (1998) cite indicate that it is the lowest achievers who gain the most from this practice. Self-assessment includes having students do the following:

- Identify their own strengths and areas for improvement. You can ask them to do this before they show their work to you for feedback, giving them prior thoughts of their own to "hang" it on—your feedback will be more meaningful and will make more sense.

- Write in a response log at the end of class, recording key points they have learned and questions they still have.

- Using established criteria, select a work sample for their portfolio that proves a certain level of proficiency, explaining why the piece qualifies.

- Offer descriptive feedback to classmates.

- Use your feedback, feedback from other students, or their own self-assessment to identify what they need to work on and set goals for future learning.

How Can I Close the Gap?

Strategy 5: Design Lessons to Focus on One Learning Target or Aspect of Quality at a Time.

When assessment information identifies a need, you can adjust instruction to target that need. In this strategy, you scaffold learning by narrowing the focus of a lesson to help students master a specific goal or to address specific misconceptions or problems.

For example, mathematics problem solving requires choosing the right strategy as one component. A science experiment lab report requires a statement of the hypothesis as one component. Writing requires an introduction as one component. Look at the components of quality and then teach them one part at a time, making sure that students understand that all of the parts ultimately must come together. You may then offer feedback focused on the component just taught, which narrows the volume of feedback students need to act on at a given time and raises their chances of success in doing so, again, especially for struggling learners. This is a time saver for you, and more instructionally powerful for students.

Strategy 6: Teach Students Focused Revision.

This is a companion to Strategy 5—when a concept, skill, or competence proves difficult for students, you can let them practice it in smaller segments, and give them feedback on just the aspects they are practicing. This strategy allows students to revise their initial work with a focus on a manageable number of learning targets or aspects of quality.

For example, show students how to revise an answer, product, or performance, and then let students revise a similar example. Begin by choosing work that needs revision on a single aspect of quality. Ask students to brainstorm advice for the (anonymous) author on how to improve the work. Then ask students, in pairs, to revise the work using their own advice. Or, ask students to write a letter to the creator of the sample, suggesting how to make it stronger for the aspect of quality discussed. You also can ask students to analyze your own work for quality and make suggestions for improvement. Revise your work using their advice, then ask them to again review it for quality. These exercises will prepare students to work on a current product or performance of their own, revising for the aspect of quality being studied. You may then give feedback on just that aspect.

Strategy 7: Engage Students in Self-reflection, and Let Them Keep Track of and Share Their Learning.

Long-term retention and motivation increase when students track, reflect on, and communicate about their learning. Any activity that requires students to look back on their journey and share their achievement with others both reinforces the learning and helps them develop insights into themselves as learners. These kinds of activities give students the opportunity to notice their own strengths, to see how far they have come, and to feel in control of the conditions of their success. By reflecting on their learning, they deepen their understanding, and will remember it longer. In addition, it is the learner, not the teacher, who is doing the work.

Here are some things you can have students do:

- Write a process paper, detailing how they solved a problem or created a product or performance. This analysis encourages them to think like professionals in your discipline.

- Write a letter to their parents about a piece of work, explaining where they are now with it and what they are trying to do next.

- Reflect on their growth: "I have become a better reader this year. I used to . . . , but now I . . ."

- Help plan and participate in conferences with parents and/or teachers to share their learning.

Action 5: Build Communication Systems That Both Support and Report Learning

It is still a common belief that report card grades and test scores represent the kind of communication needed to promote further student learning. However, they do not—they cannot. When done well, they represent summary judgments about learning success or failure. These are appropriate when the objective is to verify or report learning, such as with report card grades or annual accountability test scores. When the purpose is to support learning, feedback needs to take a different form.

Chappuis (2009) states that feedback encourages and supports student learning when it does the following:

- Focuses on attributes of the student's work rather than attributes of the student as a learner ("here is how to make your writing better" rather than "just try harder")

- Is descriptive of that work, informing the student how to do better the next time, rather than judgmental

- Is clearly understood by the intended user, leading to specific inferences as to what is needed

- Is sufficiently detailed to be helpful yet not so comprehensive as to overwhelm

- Arrives in time to inform the learning

Classroom teachers more typically tend to the more traditional communication task, that involving marks and grades. Communication that reports the sufficiency of learning should be based on sound grading practices (see O'Connor, 2007) and should satisfy the following criteria:

- Both the message sender (teacher and school) and receiver (student and parents) must understand the achievement target in question to be the same thing—if they unwittingly talk about different kinds of achievement, they will miscommunicate. This is where parent-friendly versions of the learning targets student are accountable for can play a role, and also where standards-based report cards can assist.

- The information underpinning the communication must be accurate—inaccurate information leads automatically to miscommunication. Stated another way: a bad test using bad items can do little except provide bad information in the form of student results. Further, an academic grade that factors in such variables as attendance and behavior compromises its ability to accurately communicate student learning.

- If symbols are being used to communicate student progress, schools and parents must understand them to mean the same thing—if they think the scores, symbols, or grades mean different things, communication is compromised.

- The communication must be tailored to the information needs of the intended audience. That means that, for example, schools reporting the results of a direct writing assessment, beyond providing numerical rubric scores for the traits of writing assessed would want to also include a description of those traits and/or examples of what student work looks like along the points of the rating scale.

Do Your Teachers Know How to Communicate Effectively about Student Learning?

Action 5 asks that districts and schools develop the capacity to deliver understandable and useful information about assessment *of* and assessment *for* learning results. Table 3-10 summarizes the stages of organizational preparedness to deliver effective feedback to its intended users.

Deepening Your Understanding of Balanced Communication Systems

Evaluative feedback in the form of marks or grades and summary test scores aligns with assessment *of* learning; feedback describing strengths and areas for improvement serves assessment *for* learning. Two steps you can take as a leader are to understand

Table 3-10 **Action Five: Build Communication Systems to Support and Report Student Learning**

5 Implemented	4	3 Progressing	2	1 Getting Started
We understand the value of descriptive feedback used to support learning and know that the best use of evaluative feedback is to judge the level of learning.		Some teachers in our system understand the role descriptive feedback can play in helping students learn but we have not taken systemic action to ensure it is present in every classroom.		There is no understanding of the difference between evaluative and descriptive feedback in our system or when/how each should be used.
Teachers know how to offer descriptive feedback to students that will be effective, is delivered during the learning, and is directly linked to the targets of instruction, helping to guide improvement of learning.		Some of this type of communication to students is visible, but mostly is inconsistent across the school/district.		Feedback to students is largely the traditional marks and scores that result in report card grades.
Teachers understand and apply the principles of sound grading practices, assigning report card grades that are accurate, fair, and representative of current achievement status.		We have adopted some grading practices that help support accurate report card grades but still have other practices that can lead to faulty measurement and reporting of student learning.		Each teacher grades student work based on their own system and standards.
We have developed standards-based report cards as a means to communicate student progress relative to the targets of instruction, and we provide teachers the support needed to make it work.		We have this in place in some schools/levels, but not at all levels or with the level of support needed to make it work well.		This has not yet been a focus of our work in the school/district.
Students are involved in communication about their own progress and achievement status.		We have some student/parent conferences going on, but that's about it.		No work has been done in this area.

yourself and help teachers in your school or district understand the difference between the two and the need for balance in the use of feedback, communicating both *of* and *for* learning.

A further exploration of research tells us that descriptive feedback that supports student learning—that helps them learn more—does the following:

- Points out successes and gives specific information about how to improve the performance or product (Black, Harrison, Lee, Marshall, & Wiliam, 2002; Black & Wiliam, 1998; Brown, 1994).

- Offers information about progress relative to the intended learning goal and about what action to take to reach the goal (Hattie & Timperley, 2007).

- Directs comments to the quality of the work—what was done well and what needs improving—increasing student interest in the task and level of achievement (Butler, 1988).

- Emphasizes learning goals, which leads to greater learning gains than feedback that emphasizes self-esteem (Ames, 1992; Butler, 1988; Hattie & Timperley, 2007).

- Cues the individual to direct attention to the *quality of the task* rather than to *self* (praise, effort, etc.), which appears to have a negative effect on learning. Many studies speak to effective teachers praising less than average (Cameron & Pierce, 1994; Kluger & DeNisi, 1996).

- Addresses partial understanding. When student work demonstrates lack of understanding, feedback will not help (Hattie & Timperley, 2007).

We know that parents are conditioned to the old communication/feedback model. When they see dozens of marks in a teacher's gradebook it is easy for them to confuse quantity with learning quality. Communication about student progress to them that is formative in nature doesn't reflect their own school experience, meaning leaders and teachers will need to take extra time and care in helping parents understand the role of both kinds of feedback. When they understand the shift in focus from teaching to learning, and see the effects of the use of descriptive feedback with their children they will understand the need no longer exists to put a grade on everything the student does.

Action 6: Motivate Students with Learning Success

This, the effective management of the relationship between assessment and student motivation, is the final Action in support of assessment *for* learning.

As a society and school culture, we need to examine the prevailing belief that higher levels of accountability can serve as a motivator for all students. Simply demanding higher test scores does not spur all students to try harder and learn more. Clearly, it motivates some but certainly not all—maybe not even most. Increasing anxiety works to spur action for those who already have hope of success. For those who do not, intimidation simply drives them deeper into failure.

On the other hand, a dynamic that does work as a motivator is success at learning. A personal record of academic success sets up a productive emotional response to the next set of assessment results. For students to meet standards they must believe that they can master them if they try. If they stop believing this, effort to learn will cease. What students think about and do with assessment results in some ways dictates their ultimate success, and so is every bit as important as what teachers and others do with those results.

It is helpful to remember who is in charge of the learning—it is not the teacher. Students respond in an emotionally positive way when, on seeing their results (whether high, midrange, or low) they think to themselves,

- I get it—I know what these results mean.

- I know what to do in response to do better the next time.

- I can handle this.

- I choose to keep trying.

Students respond counterproductively when their reaction to assessment results is

- I don't understand.

- I have no idea what to do about this.

- I'm probably never going to get this, anyway.

- I give up.

If students who have yet to meet standards end up here, turning up the heat through increased intimidation is exactly the wrong thing to do. If these students do not achieve some evidence of success, triggering some sense of confidence as learners, the motivation to learn will not return.

How do teachers close the gap between those who have and have not met standards if not all students believe that success is within their reach—if low achievers are giving up on themselves? The answer is, they cannot. A solution is found in applying the principles and practices of assessment *for* learning.

Do Your Teachers Use Learning Success to Motivate Students?

We have established that relying on the anxiety and intimidation of accountability to motivate learning works for some students. It can energize those who have hope of success. But for students who have experienced chronic failure, turning up the anxiety will only perpetuate that pattern. A motivator that can work is success at learning. This Action urges educators to understand these emotional dynamics as they link assessment to student motivation and success. Table 3-11 shows the stages in linking student involvement to motivation.

Table 3-11 **Action Six: Motivating Students with Learning Success**

5 Implemented	4	3 Progressing	2	1 Getting Started
Our faculty, staff, leaders, policymakers, and community understand the power student-involved assessment has to help all students experience the kind of academic success needed to remain motivated, confident, and engaged.		We are in the process of helping all stakeholders understand the motivational power of student-involved assessment *for* learning.		We largely motivate students by holding them accountable for learning.
The classroom assessment practices we use rely on student involvement in assessment during their learning to maintain their confidence and motivation.		The proportion of our teachers who involve their students in ongoing self-assessment as a motivator is increasing steadily.		Our classroom practices rarely include student-involved assessment as a motivator.

Deepening Your Understanding of How to Motivate Students with Learning Success

In his research Seligman (1998) states that optimism matters as much as talent or desire when it comes to success. Optimists see themselves as having personal control over their lives and over their decision making. When they experience defeat, they do not interpret it as a personal indictment of their capabilities, but rather as an indication that they did not use the right strategy or did not put forth enough effort at the time. For them the target is still within reach and they know that they are capable of doing better. They are in control of the situation.

On the other hand, pessimists who experience success might interpret it as a fluke. When they meet defeat, they believe that they failed because they are not capable. For them, defeat is habitual; in other words, they interpret it as personal, pervasive, and permanent. Pessimists do not see their actions paying off and feel a lack of control and a sense of helplessness.

Both sets of behaviors are learned. Teachers can help learners see that they have the ability to change situations by their own, deliberate actions, and the consistent application of principles of assessment *for* learning can help promote this.

Covington (1992), a motivational researcher, notes that self-worth theory presumes that self-acceptance is the highest human priority. In schools this often equates with one's ability to achieve. Students want to be capable learners in their own minds and want to be seen by others as capable. Again, the consistent application of assessment *for* learning strategies can help accomplish this.

Dweck (1999) states that one's beliefs about intelligence underlie success and failure. A person who believes that intelligence is malleable believes that intelligence increases through one's efforts. One does not have to worry about looking smart, but gets smart by doing. Therefore, such believers of intelligence seek out challenges and persist at them even when difficult. Using effort is seen as a means to get smarter.

Those who believe that intelligence is a fixed (unchangeable) human characteristic must protect whatever intelligence they were born with, and seek a diet of easy successes to constantly reaffirm their level of intelligence. Challenges are a threat to self-esteem, so such a person might readily pass up valuable learning opportunities. If one has to put forth a lot of effort, then one must not be smart.

Psychologists have established that the former is true—intelligence is changeable throughout the course of one's life. Teachers can help students get smarter, both in reality and in their own eyes. They can help students know what good work looks like from the beginning of their learning, help them compare their work to this standard of quality for strengths and needs, and help them learn to close the gap between the two. Teachers can help students self-assess and set goals to increase their learning or competence, giving students the tools to be in control of their own learning—to be capable, to see themselves getting smarter. Legitimate success that is visible to the student does breed success. Students do not acquire strong self-efficacy through direct efforts to raise their self-esteem, such as being told they are good students or that they are smart. Students develop strong academic confidence by being fully engaged in a task and relying on themselves as resources. It is part of the charge as their teachers to help make that happen for each of them.

Action 7: Promote the Development of Assessment Literacy

To summarize Actions 1 to 6, schools can promote learning success when they do the following:

- Make classroom assessment the foundation of a balanced assessment system.
- Have curricular roadmaps in place to guide the journey to learning success.
- Make sure all assessments produce accurate information about student learning.
- Apply assessment *for* learning strategies in the classroom.
- Balance communication systems to both support and report student learning.
- Motivate students by helping them succeed at learning.

Each of these actions requires a fundamental understanding of sound assessment practice. Typical teachers spend a quarter to a third of their available professional time engaged in assessment-related activities. If done well, students prosper, especially struggling learners. If done poorly, students suffer. But the vast majority of teachers and school leaders carry out or supervise these assessment practices without the preparation needed to assess accurately or use assessment to support student learning. And school leaders cannot provide instructional leadership in assessment without themselves understanding key principles of sound assessment

School districts must provide faculty and staff a foundational understanding of the principles of sound classroom assessment practice.

Here's an example: part of a foundation of assessment literacy is connecting clear targets to quality assessments. The ability to do that has been missing for most teachers and school leaders; neither preservice nor inservice opportunities have been provided them.

Another example: historically, teachers have mainly communicated about student learning success after arriving at summary judgment about the sufficiency of their learning—every ten weeks or semester. But again, with a new mission, everyone in the system must also support learning. This requires a different kind of communication—descriptive feedback that supports learning—and it requires the time for teachers to learn how to do this well.

Table 3-12 **Action Seven: Provide the Professional Development Needed to Ensure Assessment Literacy Throughout the System**

5 Implemented	4	3 Progressing	2	1 Getting Started
Leaders are committed to assessment literacy for all. Professional development resources have been allocated to achieve balance in our assessment systems, to have accurate assessments, and to employ assessment *for* learning practices.		We have begun to make school improvement and resource allocation decisions that reflect a desire to offer the professional development needed to form the foundation of a quality, balanced assessment system.		Such professional development is not yet a priority on our district.
Our school leaders have developed the assessment literacy they need to maintain the vision, to develop essential infrastructure, and support teacher development in assessment literacy.		We acknowledge the need to have all leaders assessment literate and leaders are finding opportunities to increase their knowledge and skills in quality, balanced assessment practices.		Assessment literacy has not been a focus of our development of school leaders.
The development of assessment literacy is offered in a professional development model that allows teachers to learn from each other in collaborative teams and practice in the classroom as they learn.		We have some teacher-directed, job-embedded staff development, but our system does not have the structures in place to support this kind of adult learning.		Our professional development model is still largely workshop based.
Professional development is having its desired impact as our program evaluation shows that we have achieved balance, a high degree of quality assessment, and an increase in student achievement.		Professional development appears to be working but we have little hard data to support that conclusion.		We are not evaluating our programs in ways that would tell us that what we do delivers results.

Do You Need to Promote the Development of Assessment Literacy?

To successfully complete Actions 1–6 school districts must provide faculty and staff a foundational understanding of the principles of sound classroom assessment practice. This Action urges the provision of professional development in assessment literacy. Table 3-12 shows the stages in implementing these opportunities.

Deepening Your Understanding of How to Promote Assessment Literacy

Learning Teams for Professional Development in Classroom Assessment

Any initiative that intends to support new learning for teachers and school leaders needs to pay as much attention to the process of the learning as it does to the content. Considerations should go beyond simply giving them the necessary tools to include attention to the conditions needed for effective adult learning and "transfer of training" into the classroom. If professional development resources in assessment literacy were allocated in your system, how might they be most effectively used? We believe that collaborative learning teams represent the future of professional development in U.S. schools. They are especially effective in schools using a professional learning community approach to school improvement. In the learning team model of professional development, teachers are provided the time and structure needed to concentrate on one topic long enough to internalize new and practical ideas for classroom use. This, combined with time to reflect on current practice and to talk with and learn from colleagues through informal coaching, makes this model of professional development effective. Participants in assessment literacy learning teams often recognize and welcome the "permission" to focus on a long-term commitment to attain classroom assessment expertise rather than assessment that centers on prepping for the state test.

By applying the principles of assessment for learning, teachers will substantiate clear research findings: doing classroom assessment right and using the results well raises student achievement.

Activity 20 in Part 4 goes into more detail on this topic, and describes what is needed for a learning team model of professional development to succeed as well as what principals can do to support learning teams.

Creating a Supportive Policy Environment

Another part of developing and maintaining a quality assessment program is a commitment to developing school or district policies that support quality assessment and that make the standards of sound assessment practice clear and understandable. While sound assessment policies don't ensure sound practices, they can contribute by reaffirming a commitment to quality.

To develop such policies at the district level, superintendents should draft for school board review and approval an assessment philosophy that spells out the assessment responsibilities for district personnel. We discuss considerations for developing sound assessment policies when we present Competency 10 in Part 4 of this Action Guide. Please note that it has been our experience that district leadership teams do the best job of analyzing and revising assessment policy after they have themselves completed a professional development program in assessment literacy.

Summarizing the Path to Excellence in Assessment

Leadership for assessment balance and quality begins with a guiding vision, showing how assessment fits into and supports instruction. School leaders should understand the importance of quality assessment at all levels and support standards of quality that will guide assessment practices in every classroom. This vision is carried out via the Seven Actions that guide district practice. Leaders must ensure an assessment-literate staff, both in the classroom and in the principal's office. The school board must establish the districtwide policy environment that will underpin the pursuit of that vision in every classroom and school within the district. District administrators must contribute clear achievement expectations that function as a unit across grade levels and disciplines, and ensure that state, district, and building assessments are used in a coordinated, aligned fashion in support of student achievement. By applying the principles of assessment *for* learning, teachers will substantiate clear research findings: doing classroom assessment right and using the results well raises student achievement.

Thinking About Assessment

Activity 5: School/District Assessment System Self-Evaluation

Purpose:

This activity is necessary in charting a path of Seven Actions that leads to your assessment vision becoming a reality. When completed, your self-evaluation will show you what parts of what Actions have been implemented and what work lies ahead of you. In effect, it helps identify priorities to be taken by your school or district, and by doing so, maps the course for achieving balance and quality.

Time:

Variable, likely to be 1–3 hours

Materials Needed:

Copies of the following School/District Assessment System Self-Evaluation (this self-evaluation also appears on the accompanying CD-ROM)

Suggested Room Setup:

- Tables and chairs set up for easy discussion among team members

- Wall space or boards for keeping a tally of the evaluation scores and for listing what is already accomplished and what needs to be addressed

Directions:

After having read in Part 3 the Seven Actions that must be addressed to have a quality, balanced assessment system and having performed a personal analysis of where your district is in the completion of those Actions, it is now time to do the self-evaluation as a leadership team.

To have everyone focused and refreshed on the Seven Actions, please view the accompanying 35-minute DVD, *Developing Balanced Assessment Systems: Seven Essential Actions for Schools and Districts*, featuring Rick Stiggins.

Read through the items in the following District Assessment System Self-Evaluation correlated to each of the Seven Actions. Discuss each item with your team and come to agreement about where you would place your school/district along the item's accompanying 5-point rating scale. Consider the following as you move through the activity:

- The larger, more diverse a team you can assemble that is representative of your school/district, the more accurate your profile is likely to be. Expanding participation in this activity to others in your system not part of your leadership study team is beneficial. Or, your team can do the profiling activity first and then repeat it with a larger group to create more understanding of the issues and gain a larger representation of opinion.

- If a larger district or school team is assembled, coming to consensus about each item may be more difficult because people will bring not only different perspectives but also very different realities. For example, one person's school may deserve a high rating on one Action while another school in the district hasn't even considered that scope of work and therefore admittedly gets a lower mark. How can that be reconciled to reflect the work the district needs to accomplish? Or, the district may be doing well overall in one area but that work has not filtered into the schools. How should the team rate the district overall? There is likely to be rich, revealing discussion about many of the issues raised in the profile; staying focused on the status of the level of analysis (school or district) is essential.

- What one knows and doesn't know when asked to make judgments or evaluations influences one's answers to questions. In this activity—as in many others in this guide—participants' responses are directly related to their level of assessment literacy.

When you have rated all Actions and summarized the results, proceed with a team discussion of your current status, using the following questions as a springboard:

- Where are our strengths—places where our ratings seem high and we think that we have made real progress? What are the keys to our success on these fronts? List them.

- What have we accomplished to date? What is still to be done? Discuss specifics.

- Where are our omissions or weaknesses—areas where we have made little or no progress to date?

- How would we rank the Actions in terms of our progress? Rank them from 1 to 7, with 7 being most completely implemented.

- For areas of little progress to date, what have been our barriers? List them.

- How can we remove these barriers? Note suggestions.

- What should be our next priorities? Which pending Actions are most critical to our specific situation? How soon can/should we act on them?

Closure:

As we noted at the start of this Action Guide, our intention is to help you in two areas: (1) at a system/organizational (school or district) level; and (2) at a personal/professional level, one that considers the necessary knowledge and skills for leading assessment reform. We think it is helpful for teams to revisit this self-evaluation profile both before and after reading and doing many of the activities in Part 4. Doing the self-evaluation now will help clarify and increase understanding of the ten competencies for leaders you will encounter there. These competencies will be beneficial in implementing the Seven Actions. Coming back after reading Part 4 and reviewing the profile in light of these ten competencies will produce a deeper, more complete self-evaluation.

School/District Assessment System Self-Evaluation

Action One: Balance the district's assessment system to meet all key user needs

Balanced assessment systems blend effective assessment use at the classroom level with interim/benchmark assessment and annual testing to serve both formative and summative purposes. This Action urges examination of current levels of balance and movement toward greater balance if needed.

5 Implemented	4	3 Progressing	2	1 Getting Started
All faculty and staff are aware of differences in assessment purpose across classroom, interim/benchmark, and annual levels, and know how to use each to support and/or verify student learning; that is, to balance formative with summative assessment. We also understand what uses can and cannot be made with each level of assessment.		There is inconsistency among staff regarding assessment purpose, and some confusion about what is formative and what is summative. We are aware of the need for balance and have begun to plan for a balanced system.		There is little understanding of differences in purpose and assessment users, or appropriate uses of results across classroom, interim/benchmark, and annual levels.
A top assessment priority is to help students develop the capacity to assess their own learning and to use assessment results to help promote further learning.		Some faculty and staff recognize that students are important users of assessment information who make data-based instructional decisions that impact their own success, and have made some progress in helping them do so.		Students have not been viewed as key assessment users and there is little awareness of the benefits of bringing them into the assessment process, or knowledge of how to do so.

School/District Assessment System Self-Evaluation *(continued)*

Action One (continued)				
5 Implemented	**4**	**3** Progressing	**2**	**1** Getting Started
We have a comprehensive assessment system in place that defines a philosophy of assessment, states the roles assessment can play, and is meeting the information needs of all users. The plan coordinates state-, district-, and building-level tests, and supports administrators and teachers in bringing assessment balance to the district and its classrooms.		We know the need to do some systemwide planning around assessment and are in the process of developing an action plan to get there.		As yet, no such system has been conceived, designed, or developed. Most of our system is made up of large-scale, standardized testing from the state level.
Policies at the district and school levels reflect the value placed on assessment balance and quality, and we have identified all of those policies that contribute to balanced and productive assessment, and have a systemic approach to the development and coordination of those policies.		We have some policies that support sound assessment practice but they are inconsistent across schools and/or at the district level. We don't always know yet what language needs to be used/replaced.		Our policies have not yet been examined for their role in supporting assessment balance and quality.
We have an information management system to collect, house, and deliver achievement information to users at classroom, interim/benchmark, and annual assessment levels.		We have an information management system but have not integrated its use across levels.		As yet no such system has been developed or purchased.
Our school board and community understand the concept and need for a balanced assessment system and are supportive of this priority.		We are currently educating our staff, policymakers, and community on the need to develop an assessment system to meet diverse information needs across levels.		Our policymakers and community are unaware of the need to think of assessment in this manner and view assessment mostly in the traditional role of measurement.

School/District Assessment System Self-Evaluation *(continued)*

Action One *(continued)*

5 Implemented	4	3 Progressing	2	1 Getting Started
We have inventoried all assessments used in the district and have categorized them by purpose, standards/targets measured, time of year, etc. for the purpose of understanding the balance we have in our current assessment system.		We are in the process of identifying all of the various assessments used at the district and school level for the purpose of getting a clearer understanding of what is currently in our assessment system.		We do not have a comprehensive picture of what assessments are currently being given.

Action Two: *Refine achievement standards to reflect clear and appropriate expectations at all levels*

Achievement standards are fundamental to any assessment system. That is, clear learning targets are needed to underpin classroom, interim/benchmark, and annual assessments. This Action calls for developing local achievement expectations as a foundation for balanced assessment.

5 Implemented	4	3 Progressing	2	1 Getting Started
We continue to refine our local achievement standards, have aligned them with state standards, and have identified our highest-priority learning outcomes.		We are aware of the need to develop clear local academic standards aligned to state standards and are in the process of doing so. What is in place is not yet used consistently across classrooms.		Local learning expectations are not in place.
Assessment results for all uses are always linked back to the local content standards.		We can link some assessments back to our written curriculum, but don't always know how or why we should do that.		We use the results as they are delivered to us and have yet to take the extra step of consistently matching results to the written curriculum.
We have deconstructed our standards into knowledge, reasoning, performance skills, and product development learning targets at each grade level for each subject.		We are in the process of deconstructing each of our standards into the scaffolding of grade-level curricula.		The deconstruction process has not been initiated.

School/District Assessment System Self-Evaluation *(continued)*

Action Two *(continued)*				
5 Implemented	**4**	**3** Progressing	**2**	**1** Getting Started
We have transformed the grade- and course-level learning targets that guide classroom assessment and instruction into student- and family-friendly versions.		Some of that work has been accomplished but we have not completed it for all grade levels and courses or it is not adequately communicated to parents and/or students.		We have yet to begin this process.
We have verified that each teacher in each classroom is master of the content standards that their students are expected to master. We provide professional support in content areas to teachers when needed.		We have identified contexts in which professional development is needed to ensure teacher competence in terms of our standards and that learning is underway.		There has been no investigation of teacher preparedness in their own content area(s).
All teachers in the district have received adequate training and ongoing support in developing their understanding of the written curricular documents. Teachers are given time to collaboratively plan lessons aimed at accomplishing grade-level/subject expectations.		We share curricular documents with our teachers. If there are questions about the new curriculum we address them, and provide some training at the beginning of the year in the understanding and use of those documents.		The curricular documents are available on request or are given to teachers when the documents have undergone revisions.
A curriculum implementation plan is in place to ensure consistency in achievement expectations across classrooms. Teachers are held accountable for teaching the written curriculum.		We recognize a need for a curriculum implementation plan to ensure the written curriculum is the taught curriculum, and have taken some steps to ensure that.		We have not ensured that there is consistency in achievement expectations across teachers. What is taught in each classroom in the same subject/grade level can differ widely.
Model/sample lessons and assessments, linked to the content standards, are available and used for professional development.		This is true for some subjects and grade levels.		We do not have this in our school/district.

School/District Assessment System Self-Evaluation *(continued)*

> *Action Three: Ensure assessment quality in all contexts to support good decision making*
>
> Because a variety of decisions are made based on assessment results, all assessments at classroom, interim/benchmark, and annual levels of use must yield dependable information about student achievement. This Action urges the evaluation of current assessments to verify quality.

5 Implemented	4	3 Progressing	2	1 Getting Started
We have adopted and can apply the criteria by which we should judge the quality of our assessments, both *of* and *for* learning.		We have standards for assessment quality, and some district staff have the capability to evaluate for quality, but it is not a consistent condition in the district.		No such criteria have been identified; no quality control framework exists for us at any level.
There is general understanding that quality assessments form the foundation for accurate report card grades and for decisions made about students that rely on assessment data.		We subscribe to the use of multiple measures but haven't ensured that all data sources yield dependable results.		We've not considered this as a priority for our time/resources.
At the classroom level, teachers understand the importance of selecting the appropriate assessment method match to the type(s) of learning target to be assessed in order to help ensure quality results.		Teachers understand the need to vary assessment methods but may not apply strict quality criteria when doing so.		Teachers do not see the link between assessment quality and the assessment method used.
We have conducted a local evaluation of the quality of all of our assessments, including interim/benchmark and common assessments, if used.		We are aware of the need to conduct such an evaluation and are planning to conduct it.		There is no awareness of the need for or plans to conduct such an evaluation.

School/District Assessment System Self-Evaluation *(continued)*

Action Four: Help learners become assessors by using assessment for learning strategies in the classroom

By involving students in their own assessment during learning, teachers can maximize their confidence, motivation, and achievement. This Action urges that teachers involve them in assessment, understanding them as users of results just as they do themselves and others.

5 Implemented	4	3 Progressing	2	1 Getting Started
Faculty, staff, policymakers, and community members all understand and embrace the idea of assessment *for* learning—i.e., student-involved assessment to promote learning.		We are in the process of building local awareness of and belief in this set of ideas. Formative assessment is visible, but not as assessment *for* learning.		As yet, there is no awareness of the value of this concept or set of classroom practices.
Teachers use assessment information to focus instruction day to day in the classroom and communicate learning expectations to students in language they can understand.		Our primary use of formative assessment is at the interim or common assessment level, not exactly day-to-day at the classroom level. Some teachers know how to translate learning targets into student-friendly language, but many do not.		This has not been a focus or priority for us to date.
Teachers design assessments to help students self-assess and to help them use assessment results as feedback to set goals.		Some teachers administer assessments as practice; others need training to help them make that transition.		We don't involve students in the assessment process in these ways.

School/District Assessment System Self-Evaluation *(continued)*

Action Five: Build communication systems to support and report student learning

Action 5 asks that districts and schools develop the capacity to deliver useful and understandable information about assessment *of* and assessment *for* learning results.

5 Implemented	4	3 Progressing	2	1 Getting Started
We understand the value of descriptive feedback used to support learning and know that the best use of evaluative feedback is to judge the level of learning.		Some teachers in our system understand the role descriptive feedback can play in helping students learn but we have not taken systemic action to ensure it is present in every classroom.		There is no understanding of the difference between evaluative and descriptive feedback in our system or when/how each should be used.
Teachers know how to offer descriptive feedback to students that will be effective, is delivered during the learning, and is directly linked to the targets of instruction, helping to guide improvement of learning.		Some of this type of communication to students is visible, but mostly is inconsistent across the school/district.		Feedback to students is largely the traditional marks and scores that result in report card grades.
Teachers understand and apply the principles of sound grading practices, assigning report card grades that are accurate, fair, and representative of current achievement status.		We have adopted some grading practices that help support accurate report card grades but still have other practices that can lead to faulty measurement and reporting of student learning.		Each teacher grades student work based on their own system and standards.
We have developed standards-based report cards as a means to communicate student progress relative to the targets of instruction, and we provide teachers the support needed to make it work.		We have this in place in some schools/levels, but not at all levels or with the level of support needed to make it work well.		This has not yet been a focus of our work in the school/district.
Students are involved in communication about their own progress and achievement status.		We have some student/parent conferences going on, but that's about it.		No work has been done in this area.

School/District Assessment System Self-Evaluation *(continued)*

Action Six: Motivate students with learning success

The practice of relying on the anxiety and intimidation of accountability to motivate learning works for some students. It can energize those who have hope of success. But for students who have experienced chronic failure, turning up the anxiety will drive them more deeply into academic failure. For all students, a motivator that can work is success at learning. This Action urges educators to understand these emotional dynamics as they link assessment to student motivation and success.

5 Implemented	4	3 Progressing	2	1 Getting Started
Our faculty, staff, leaders, policymakers, and community understand the power student-involved assessment has to help all students experience the kind of academic success needed to remain motivated, confident, and engaged.		We are in the process of helping all stakeholders understand the motivational power of student-involved assessment *for* learning.		We largely motivate students by holding them accountable for learning.
The classroom assessment practices we use rely on student involvement in assessment during their learning to maintain their confidence and motivation.		The proportion of our teachers who involve their students in ongoing self-assessment as a motivator is increasing steadily.		Our classroom practices rarely include student-involved assessment as a motivator.

School/District Assessment System Self-Evaluation *(continued)*

Action Seven: *Provide the professional development needed to ensure assessment literacy throughout the system*

To successfully complete Actions 1–6 school districts must provide faculty and staff a foundational understanding of the principles of sound classroom assessment practice. This Action urges the provision of professional development in assessment literacy.

5 Implemented	4	3 Progressing	2	1 Getting Started
Leaders are committed to assessment literacy for all. Professional development resources have been allocated to achieve balance in our assessment systems, to have accurate assessments, and to employ assessment *for* learning practices.		We have begun to make school improvement and resource allocation decisions that reflect a desire to offer the professional development needed to form the foundation of a quality, balanced assessment system.		Such professional development is not yet a priority on our district.
Our school leaders have developed the assessment literacy they need to maintain the vision, to develop essential infrastructure, and support teacher development in assessment literacy.		We acknowledge the need to have all leaders assessment literate and leaders are finding opportunities to increase their knowledge and skills in quality, balanced assessment practices.		Assessment literacy has not been a focus of our development of school leaders.
The development of assessment literacy is offered in a professional development model that allows teachers to learn from each other in collaborative teams and practice in the classroom as they learn.		We have some teacher-directed, job-embedded staff development, but our system does not have the structures in place to support this kind of adult learning.		Our professional development model is still largely workshop based.
Professional development is having its desired impact as our program evaluation shows that we have achieved balance, a high degree of quality assessment, and an increase in student achievement.		Professional development appears to be working but we have little hard data to support that conclusion.		We are not evaluating our programs in ways that would tell us that what we do delivers results.

PART 4

Required Skills for Assessment Balance and Quality

STUDENT
SUCCESS

Teacher
Competencies

Planning
for
Action

Required Skills
for Assessment
Balance and Quality

The Path to Assessment
Balance and Quality

Building the Vision

Laying the Foundation

The Building Blocks of Assessment Success

Required Skills for Assessment Balance and Quality

4

S o far, we've explored a vision for a balanced, quality assessment system and have outlined Seven Actions to help put that system in place. We described what each Action looks like, asked you to analyze your organization relative to each one, and provided considerations and suggestions for implementing them. In Part 4 we turn our attention to ten specific assessment competencies for school leaders that will assist in deepening understanding of the Seven Actions, and provide a foundation of professional knowledge and skills that help make the Actions achievable. The Ten Competencies are listed in Figure 4-1.

Leading Assessment *for* Learning

Current research shows that, of all school-related factors that influence student learning, only classroom instruction has greater impact than leadership. As noted in the 2008 ISLLC standards, leaders have the greatest impact when they set direction, citing that the goals and purpose they provide serve to strengthen and solidify the faculty.

This framework of competencies for school leaders is specific largely to the classroom level of assessment in a balanced system. There are two reasons we have focused the content of the framework at this level. First, standards-driven reform has created new knowledge requirements and responsibilities for school leaders. In today's systems, the practice of sorting students along a bell curve, and thus artificially creating winners and losers, is replaced by a mission that all students must learn well. Instead of a curriculum focused on what a teacher should teach, the curriculum identifies what students must know and be able to do. These standards are public, and communicate what a state or district values when it comes to student learning. Assessing the standards, not just through large-scale accountability tests or even local short-cycle or common assessments, but day to day in the classroom where standards, instruction, and assessment are all pages in the same book, is a requirement for effective standards-based reform.

Figure 4-1   **Ten Assessment Competencies for School Leaders**

1. The leader understands the attributes of a sound and balanced assessment system, and the conditions required to achieve balance in local systems.

2. The leader understands the necessity of clear academic achievement standards, aligned classroom-level achievement targets, and their relationship to the development of accurate assessments.

3. The leader understands the standards of quality for student assessments, helps teachers learn to assess accurately, and ensures that these standards are met in all school/district assessments.

4. The leader knows assessment *for* learning practices and works with staff to integrate them into classroom instruction.

5. The leader creates the conditions necessary for the appropriate use and reporting of student achievement information, and can communicate effectively with all members of the school community about student assessment results, including report card grades, and their relationship to improving curriculum and instruction.

6. The leader understands the issues related to the unethical and inappropriate use of student assessment and protects students and staff from such misuse.

7. The leader can plan, present and/or secure professional development activities that contribute to the use of sound assessment practices.

8. The leader knows and can evaluate the teacher's classroom assessment competencies, and helps teachers learn to assess accurately and use the results to benefit student learning.

9. The leader analyzes student assessment information accurately, uses the information to improve curriculum and instruction, and assists teachers in doing the same.

10. The leader develops and implements sound assessment and assessment-related policies.

The second reason this leadership framework is focused largely on the classroom level of assessment is the reward in improved student learning brought about by the use of classroom assessment *for* learning. Described by Fullan (2004) as "a high-yield strategy," the research reported on the topic (discussed in Part 2) helps explain why leadership knowledge and skill specific to it are beneficial. Assessment *for* learning has implications not just for school leaders but also for broader educational practice: the research is conclusive, and improved learning lies within the grasp of anyone wishing to apply it.

What does it look like when school leaders demonstrate mastery of the Ten Assessment Competencies? We have included examples, learning activities, and opportunities for practice as well as success indicators for each competency. There are more ways to work toward the Ten Competencies than we have included—we provide a start, a catalyst for you to think about ways that you can be an instructional leader in assessment. From there, you can reflect on what you already know and can do, and on what you need to do or learn next.

Competency 1

The leader understands the attributes of a sound and balanced assessment system, and the conditions required to achieve balance in local systems.

Assessment-literate school leaders know what to do to bring balance and quality to their local assessment system. First, they attend to the balance of assessments *of* learning, those that check achievement status at a given point in time, including both classroom status checks and those conducted using standardized tests, with classroom assessments *for* learning, assessments specifically designed to involve students and to inform them about their own progress. Each requires its own support resources, professional development, and integration into school improvement. Second, they look for a balance of achievement targets. If the grade level or course curriculum derived from state standards predominantly reflects knowledge targets at the expense of more complex reasoning and skill targets, an imbalance in what students learn results. Third, they monitor balance of assessment methods (selected response, written response, performance assessment, and personal communication), achieved in part through a proper balance of learning targets in the written curriculum. Fourth, they ensure a balance of communication methods, which allows students, parents, and other stakeholders to gain access to timely and understandable information about student achievement.

> *Assessment-literate school leaders know what to do to bring balance and quality to their local assessment system.*

In a nutshell, they seek balance in the following:

- Assessment purpose
- Achievement targets
- Assessment methods
- Communication methods

School leaders also need to examine the balance and relationship between what is assessed at the state and at local levels. The state testing program may seem so comprehensive that the need for a local assessment system may not be apparent. However, just as classroom assessment is not likely to meet all information needs regarding attainment of state and district standards, by the same token, the state's assessment system may not provide all the information district decision makers need about student achievement. Especially in a time of heavy focus on accountability testing, leaders need to ensure that state and local systems are working in concert to afford useful information about state and local achievement priorities.

Success Indicators for Competency 1

The leader

- Can articulate a vision of excellence in assessment that calls for balance, accurate assessment, and assessment *for* learning.

- Knows the differences among and the appropriate uses of classroom, interim/ benchmark, and annual assessment, including the key decisions to be made, the decision makers, and the kinds of information needed to inform those decisions.

- Uses the results of the self-analysis in Part 3 to create an action plan for progress toward a system built on balance and quality.

Practice with Competency 1

Look at your district action plan or campus improvement plan; is there any mention, beyond the use of data, of the various sources of the data? If not, what could be added to improve the balance of sources of assessment information?

Create a graphic representation of the necessary components in a balanced assessment system depicting how each component contributes to the system.

What does your school or district do now that helps balance the type of achievement information parents receive about their students?

Thinking About Assessment

Activity 6: Merging Local and State Assessment Systems

Purpose:

We've advocated that a local assessment program function as a system, with each component sharing a clear purpose, all working toward the same goal of improved student learning. The system must meet the informational needs of all users of assessment. This activity extends the systems-thinking approach to assessment by asking team members to consider what is necessary to achieve a level of balance and synergy between state and local assessment systems.

Time:

1 hour

Materials Needed:

- The grids from the assessment audit of your district in Activity 4

- Information on your state assessment(s)—test and item specifications, test examples or methods, sample reports distributed at the district, school, teacher, and student levels

Suggested Room Setup:

- Tables and chairs set for ease of discussion among participants

- Interactive whiteboards or easels with flipcharts and markers to record discussion and decision making

Directions:

First, gather the grids your team used to conduct your assessment audit in Activity 4. That activity helped map the "big picture" of assessment in your school or district. In addition, gather information about the state assessment system, including test and item specifications if available, examples of the various assessments and methods used, and sample reports from state assessments to the various levels: district, school, teacher, and student. Remember that it is difficult for any single test to deliver accurate, reliable, and meaningful information if the test is spread too thinly among multiple purposes. With this information, consider the following questions:

- What is (are) the purpose(s) of the state test(s)?

- Considering your big picture, what specific summative (accountability) decisions need to be made based on assessment results and who is making them?

- Of these, which can be informed by state assessment results? Which cannot?

- Again, consider your big picture. What specific formative applications (supporting student learning) need to be informed by assessment results and who is making those decisions?

- Which of these can and cannot be informed by state assessment results?

Now go back to the "big picture" of assessment in your school/district once again in relation to your answers to the above questions. If there are information needs the state tests do not meet, are they being met currently by district, school, or classroom assessments? Are there subjects that seem overtested while others are not tested at all? Is there redundancy among state, district, and school assessments?

What information should your local assessment system provide? To whom? For what purposes? Answers to these questions can guide your choices of what to test locally and how to test it.

Closure:

No doubt your team could pose other questions about how to get the most from a system that integrates state and local assessment. You might address balance in standards or targets tested, assessment methods used, or methods for communicating the information to the users. You could also look at balance from the summative/formative perspective; are students getting opportunities to practice before having to show what they know for an accountability purpose? Our purpose in this activity is to illustrate the opportunity local leaders have to improve balance and quality, even if the state system might drive the majority of public focus and attention.

Thinking About Assessment

Activity 7: Auditing for Balance in Classroom Assessment

Purpose:

When introduced to a new standards-aligned curriculum, teachers swiftly and accurately identify the primary roadblock to implementation: "When am I going to find time to teach *all this*?" The following activity provides a process by which teachers can compare what they currently teach and assess to the content of a new curriculum, in order to determine the following:

- Where their instruction and assessment already align

- What parts of the new curriculum they need to insert

- Which instructional activities and assessments they can eliminate

Is there balance among the written curriculum targets and the assessment methods used to assess them?

To complete the activity, teachers need to have created their current personal curriculum map for the year or course, including the content and skills they will teach and assessments they will use for each.

Time:

2–3 hours, depending on the scope of the comparison

Materials Needed:

- Each teacher's current curriculum map for the year or course, including content and skills taught and assessments used

- Numbered list of the new district curriculum standards/grade-level learning targets for each subject to be addressed

Suggested Room Setup:
- Tables and chairs set for ease of discussion among participants
- Interactive whiteboards or easels with flipcharts and markers to record discussion and decision making

Directions:

Data Gathering

1. *New and current curriculum—Where's the match?* Compare your curriculum map's list of content and skills to the numbered list of the new curriculum standards/grade-level learning targets. On your curriculum map, highlight those content and skill entries that show up on the list. Next, go back through the highlighted content and skill entries and write the number of the new curriculum standard(s)/grade-level learning target(s) next to each highlighted content and skill on your curriculum map to show the match.

2. *Instruction—How's the balance?* Working with the content and skill entries you highlighted on your curriculum map in Step 1, determine the amount of emphasis each new standard or grade-level learning target receives in your current teaching. Is it about right, given its relative importance to everything else students must learn, and its emphasis in state and district assessments? Is it overrepresented? Underrepresented? Not present at all? Mark the corresponding column on the chart, "Comparing the Classroom Curriculum to District/State Standards," page 105 (a version suitable for writing in appears on the accompanying CD-ROM).

3. *Assessment—How's the balance?* Again working with the content and skill entries you highlighted in Step 1, refer to the assessments students take over the course of the year. Is each new standard or grade-level learning target sufficiently sampled, given its relative importance to everything else students must learn, and its emphasis in state and district assessments? Is it oversampled? Undersampled? Or, not assessed at all? Mark the corresponding column on the chart, "Comparing the Classroom Curriculum to District/State Standards."

Decision Making

4. *What to leave out?* Examine the content and skills you **didn't** highlight in Step 1 to determine which can and should be eliminated from your curriculum map. If you can address the new curriculum in less than the full year, consider which of these content and skills can and should remain in your teaching plan.

5. *What to adjust?* Use the information on the chart, "Comparing the Classroom Curriculum to District/State Standards" gathered in Steps 2 and 3, to rework your curriculum map.

Comparing the Classroom Curriculum to District/State Standards

Standard/ Grade- Level Learning Target	Instruction and Activities				Assessment			
	Right amount of emphasis	Too much emphasis	Not enough emphasis	Not present	Sufficient sample	Oversampled	Undersampled	Not sampled
1.								
2.								
3.								
4.								
5.								
6.								
7.								

Competency 2

The leader understands the necessity of clear academic achievement standards, aligned classroom-level achievement targets, and their relationship to the development of accurate assessments.

Many students come to school every day prepared to learn yet are not given a clear sense of what is being asked of them. Those who cannot clearly see the target will have difficulty hitting it. Students learn more when they know what they are expected to achieve. Many teachers are adrift in a sea of standards; they have state standards, supporting curriculum frameworks, grade-level and subject-area documents, and curriculum guides aligning standards to textbook material. But if they are not given the training, support, and time needed to transfer it all into everyday teaching, the written curriculum will not become the taught curriculum (Schmoker, 2002).

It is fair to assume that if the curriculum floor of the house is in disarray then the assessment floor is going to be equally messy. The fact that the district or school might already have a written curriculum may or may not be enough. Competency 2 asks leaders to ensure that classroom instruction aims directly at the written curriculum, and that learning targets are made clear to all stakeholders: teachers, students, and parents.

- To what extent is the written curriculum implemented in each classroom?
- Is it intentionally and effectively aligned with state standards?
- Does it represent or identify highest-priority learning standards?
- Have those standards been sufficiently deconstructed into the classroom-level targets that students must achieve to obtain mastery of those standards? (See Activity 10 for practice in this area.)
- Is there a match between what is taught and what is tested at all levels, between what is written and what is learned?
- Is it a high-quality curriculum, written with clarity and at a level of specificity to guide instruction?
- Is the curriculum balanced among the four different types of learning targets (knowledge, reasoning, skill, product), resulting in the use of a variety of assessment methods?

It is also important to ensure the curriculum is available to parents and students in versions written specifically for them. Curriculum documents translated to everyday language and in a user-friendly format can be posted on the refrigerator at home, and help parents not only know what their children are learning but support them in that effort. Leaders demonstrate Competency 2 when they support teachers in curriculum mapping (see Jacobs, 1997) or grade-level/subject-area articulation activities to further clarify what is taught and assessed, and when they provide structured time for teachers to work together to develop lessons geared toward the standards and aligned assessments.

In addition, as discussed in Action 2 in Part 3 of this guide, it is essential for leaders to ensure that all teachers are masters of the content knowledge they are assigned to teach. Effective leaders arrange for subject-area professional development where needed and institute hiring practices that place a high priority on selecting candidates with strong backgrounds in curricular content.

Other ways leaders can demonstrate this competency include the following:

- Verify that content standards drive classroom instruction and that daily lessons deliver the scaffolding students need to attain mastery of those standards as reflected on assessments *of* learning.

- Break down group achievement data into standard-by-standard information, so they can report individual student progress based on those same content standards.

- Ensure instruction is aimed at all targets in the written curriculum, not just those assessed by the state for accountability purposes.

Success Indicators for Competency 2

The leader

- Knows why clear achievement targets underpin a quality assessment system, can outline the attributes of quality standards, and knows how to ensure quality in local assessments.

- Can communicate the roles of both summative and formative assessment in standards-based schools.

- Values the transformation of learning targets into student- and family-friendly versions and can describe a process to transform them.

Practice with Competency 2

Explain to a colleague the process of deconstructing standards, including examples of the various kinds of classroom learning targets. Describe why this is an important function and how it is related to quality assessment. (See Activity 10.)

Discuss with a teacher the process for transforming one of their important learning targets into student-friendly language and the benefits of doing so. (See Activity 13.)

Thinking About Assessment

Activity 8: Embracing the Vision of a Standards-based School

Purpose:

Embracing the vision of a standards-based school might be difficult for some, both staff members and others in the community. In most adults' student experience, moving to the next grade was based on seat time and doing passing work on tests and activities in the subject areas. In a standards-based school student success is contingent on mastering a set of standards that progress through the grades until students reach mastery on the standards for graduation in various content areas. In this activity leaders consider what it will take to help all members of the school system adopt a universal vision of standards-based schooling.

Time:

30 minutes

Materials Needed:

Materials to record the discussion

Suggested Room Setup:

Tables and chairs for easy discussion among participants

Directions:

As leaders, determine what talking points to share with teachers, parents, and your community to help them understand what a standards-based school is and what it means for the students who attend it, for the adults who work in it, and for the parents and the community who support it. Considering the following questions will assist you:

- What is a standards-based school and how is it the same and different from the schools of our past?

- If mastery of the standards that progress to graduation is necessary for our students, what implications does this have for the following:

  1. The written curriculum that is developed
  2. The use of the written curriculum in the classrooms
  3. The assessments that are developed and used
  4. The instruction used with students
  5. Reporting and grading students' learning
  6. Hiring new teachers
  7. Evaluating teaching
  8. Determining needed professional development
  9. Determining when a student progresses to the next level of standards
  10. The assistance provided to students who have difficulty progressing

- Noting the implications, what beliefs that people currently have about their schools will have to be addressed?

- Noting the implications, what professional development, new learning, or other processes will be necessary to embrace this new vision of a standards-based school?

  1. By the students
  2. By the teachers
  3. By the parents
  4. By the community
  5. By you as leaders

 Thinking About Assessment

Activity 9: Implementing the Written Curriculum

Purpose:

The written curriculum must be uniformly implemented to increase the probability that the learning expectations for students are consistent across schools and classrooms. Ensuring implementation and continued use of district-adopted curricula in every classroom of the school district is a responsibility best shared. The roles-based plan outlined here defines responsibilities for each member of your school's or district's education team. This activity provides ideas on how different roles/positions in the organization can help make the written curriculum of the state, district, or school be what is used to plan and deliver instruction.

Time:

Variable

Materials Needed:

Information or documents detailing the level of curriculum implementation in your school/district

Suggested Room Setup:

Tables and chairs for easy discussion among members of the curriculum committee

Directions:

1. Gather information on the level of curriculum implementation in your school or district. There may be uniformity in certain schools and not others, in certain grade levels and departments and not others, or implementation issues may exist systemwide. Some teachers may already use the written curriculum for its intended purpose, others may have used curriculum mapping to increase teacher ownership as well as clarity of the learning targets.

2. We suggest that you use the following lists of responsibilities as the basis for self-study—to see if all roles are being fulfilled. If they are not, determine what needs to be done and by whom to guarantee quality implementation in every school. You can do this by discussing with your administrative team or curriculum committee to what extent each function has been carried by the specific role/job title.

Curriculum Office:

- Make the written curriculum readily available in multiple ways and easily read for all subjects, all grade levels, K–12.

- Provide ongoing training for teachers in understanding and teaching all learning targets.

- Provide targeted training for teachers new to the district.

- Provide "at a glance" sheets to teachers and within public documents such as parent handbooks to use with parents during back-to-school nights, conferences, etc.

- Provide skill continuum documents over grade-level spans when appropriate.

- Provide evidence that the new curriculum improves student learning.

- Provide sample classroom assessments and tasks linked to the written curriculum.

- Carefully review all instructional materials for clear alignment and support of the written curriculum.

- Ensure alignment of local curriculum with state standards.

Building Principal:

- Focus supervision and evaluation of classroom teaching on use of the curriculum in planning and delivering instruction and in assessing student progress.

- Frequently observe the curriculum in action in the classroom.

- Use the written curriculum as the foundation for intervention and student assistance programs.

- Provide teachers common planning time to work together to plan lessons leading to the accomplishment of the standards.

- Act as conduit between Curriculum Office and school staff.

- Promote use of the written curriculum through personal knowledge of the specific objectives.

- Help connect and align adopted curriculum with classroom practice through staff development, faculty meetings, vertical teaming groups, etc.

- Help secure resources for teachers to help understand/teach the curriculum, as needed.

- Call on curriculum specialists or master teachers to assist as necessary.

- Encourage teachers to follow a process to "audit" classroom curriculum against the adopted curriculum, if necessary.

- Help ensure instructional materials support the written curriculum.

Classroom Teacher:

- Teach and assess the written curriculum.

- Use district documents as the basis for daily planning and formative and summative assessment.

- Communicate the learning expectations to students and parents, regularly and in student- and parent-friendly language.

- Possess detailed knowledge of subject-area objectives and be able to classify the type of learning target.

- Monitor each student's progress toward the content standards.

- In summary: know it, teach it, and assess it.

School Board Policies:

- Develop curriculum implementation policy.

- Align district policies/curriculum to state goals.

- Ensure professional development policies support subject-specific training.

Others: (department heads, learning specialists, management team, etc.)

- Site-based teams support and problem-solve implementation issues.

In addition, the following functions have roles to play in implementing the written curriculum:

Staff Development:

- Clearly focus on curriculum implementation through a common training model for schools to follow.

- In instrumental strategies training, use essential learning as context/examples.

- Offer professional development in content areas, linked to identified standards/curriculum.

- Continue teacher involvement in curriculum revision/improvement.

- Provide school-based training on units of study based on the curriculum.

- Develop enrichment units/lessons and distribute them.

- Continue training related to specific curricula.

- Offer teachers an audit of building/classroom materials to ensure curriculum alignment.

Teacher Evaluation:

- Continue to encourage staff to write professional growth goals related to curriculum implementation for formative evaluation.

- Summative evaluation criteria/indicators relate to planning lessons, teaching, and assessing the written curriculum.

- Pre/post conferences always focus in part on the intended learning, as drawn from the written curriculum.

Curriculum Documents:	Texts/Supplemental Materials:
• Readily available, user friendly, similar formats for all subjects.	• Must align with and support standards and grade-level curriculum.
• Curriculum at-a-glance documents provided.	• Require appropriate level of introduction/training for teachers.
• Aligned to state standards.	
• Available electronically through district website as well as hard copy.	
• Parent- and student-friendly version provided.	
Special Education, LAP, Title 1:	**Reporting Student Progress and Student Work:**
• IEPs (academic portion) and LAP instructional plans need to be tied to district curriculum.	• Link report card phrases to the written curriculum to ensure standards-based reporting.

Thinking About Assessment

Activity 10: Deconstructing Standards into Classroom-level Achievement Targets: Practice for School Leaders

Purpose:

The goal of state standards is to set priorities on what students need to know and be able to do. Sometimes standards are broken down into benchmarks or indicators to further define these priorities. But, have you ever looked at content standards, benchmarks, or indicators and still been confused about what they meant?

• What am I going to teach here?

• How do I explain the target to students?

• Will my colleagues interpret this the same as I do?

• What do I do to enable students to do well on this?

No matter how carefully their creators list, describe, and break down content standards, many still must be translated into daily classroom teaching activities. We've found that when content standards are not accompanied by what can serve as day-to-day classroom curriculum, it's helpful to "deconstruct," or break down, unclear standards to see what knowledge, reasoning proficiencies, skills, and/or products underpin student success. Classroom instruction and assessment is then built around these "deconstructed" learning targets. This activity is designed to provide an example of a process for deconstructing standards and classifying learning targets. It serves as only an introduction, an illustration of the value of the process. We recommend more in-depth practice than we can provide here.

Time:

1 hour

Materials Needed:

- Interactive whiteboard or flipcharts, markers

- Copies of standards, benchmarks, or indicators, or whatever level of curriculum that seems vague or unclear to teachers

Suggested Room Setup:

Tables and chairs set so teachers can discuss and record their work

The Process:

1. Choose a standard, indicator, or benchmark that is unclear—where it isn't immediately clear what you might teach, or where teachers might have different interpretations of what the indicator might mean. For example, "Knows the binomial theorem" might mean

   a. Knowledge interpretations: (1) Knows it by sight—can pick it out of a list. (2) Can reproduce it when asked.

   b. Reasoning interpretations: (1) Can use it to solve a problem when instructed to do so. (2) Can choose the problems best solved using the binomial theorem. (3) Can write a problem that would require the binomial theorem to solve.

Each of these interpretations would have different implications for instruction. Which interpretation is correct?

2. For your chosen standard, identify whether it is, ultimately, a knowledge, reasoning, skills, or product learning target. Each of these is defined in the accompanying list, "Types of Achievement Targets."

3. To help determine the "ultimate" target type of a particular benchmark, look for key words. Key words are shown in Table 4-1, "Types of Achievement Targets—Key Words." For example, identify the "ultimate" type of each of the following standards:

   - Identify words that have similar meanings (synonyms).

   - Use clear diction, pitch, tempo, and tone, and adjust volume and tempo to stress important ideas.

Types of Achievement Targets

Use this list to help you understand and identify the different kinds of classroom learning to be developed and assessed as students work toward achieving state standards:

Master Factual and Procedural *Knowledge*

Some to be learned outright

Some to be retrieved using reference materials

Use Knowledge to *Reason* and Solve Problems

Analytical or comparative reasoning

Synthesizing

Classifying

Induction and deduction

Critical/evaluative thinking

Demonstrate Mastery of Specific *Skills*

Speaking a second language

Giving an oral presentation

Working effectively on a team

Science process skills

Create Quality *Products*

Writing samples

Term projects

Artistic products

Research reports

Shop projects

Science exhibits

Acquire Positive *Affect/Dispositions*

Desire to learn/read/think critically

Positive attitude toward school

Good citizenship

Respect toward self and others

Flexibility

Perseverance

- Keep records of investigations and observations that are understandable weeks or months later.

- Identify which hypotheses are valuable even though they are not supported.

- Classify ideas from informational texts as main ideas or supporting details.

- Model a problem situation using physical materials.

- Write, simplify, and evaluate algebraic expressions (including formulas) to generalize situations and solve problems.

- Evaluate policies that have been proposed as ways of dealing with social changes resulting from new technologies.

(Answers: knowledge, skill, product, knowledge, reasoning, product, knowledge or reasoning, knowledge or reasoning.)

Note: Key words won't always identify the "ultimate" target type of a standard, indicator, or benchmark. For example, what is the ultimate goal of "Knows the binomial theorem"? The word *knows* indicates that it's a knowledge target, but is it really ultimately a reasoning target? Since there may be ambiguity on "ultimate" type, the first job is to come to agreement on what the standard, benchmark, or indicator means.

4. Next, consider the knowledge, reasoning, and/or skills prerequisite to and un-derpinning competence of your selected standard, benchmark, or indicator. Ask yourself the following four questions. (Don't list every little piece of knowledge or minor skill, just the major ones.)

- What does a student need to know and understand to attain mastery on this benchmark?

- What patterns of reasoning, if any, are required to attain mastery on this benchmark?

- On what specific performance skills, if any, must students attain proficiency to attain mastery on this benchmark?

- What products, if any, would students be proficient in creating if they were masters of this benchmark?

These form a hierarchy. If the ultimate type of target is "product," then it has all four types of underpinnings: knowledge, reasoning, skills, and products. However, if the standard is ultimately a skill, then there will be only knowledge, reasoning, and skill underpinnings. Likewise, if the standard is ultimately reasoning, there will be only knowledge and reasoning underpinnings. And, like the nursery rhyme, knowledge stands alone.

Table 4-1 **Types of Achievement Targets—Key Words**

Target Type	Explanation	Content Standards/ Benchmark Key Words	Examples
Knowledge/ Understanding	Some knowledge/facts/concepts to be learned outright; some to be retrieved using reference materials	Explain, understand, describe, identify, recognize, tell, name, list, give examples, define, label, match, choose, recall, recognize, select	Vocabulary Measurement concepts U.S. government structure
Reasoning	Thinking proficiencies; using one's knowledge to solve a problem, make a decision, plan, etc.	*Analyze*: components, parts, ingredients, logical sequence, steps, main idea, supporting details, determine, dissect, examine, order *Compare/contrast*: discriminate between/among; alike and different, relate, distinguish between *Synthesize*: combine into, blend, formulate, organize, adapt, modify *Classify*: categorize, sort, group *Infer/deduce*: interpret, implications, predict, draw conclusions *Evaluate*: justify, support opinion, think critically, debate, defend, dispute, evaluate, judge, prove	Think critically Analyze authors' use of language Solve problems Compare forms of government Self-evaluation Analyze health information
Skills	Behavioral demonstrations; where the doing is what is important; using one's knowledge and reasoning to perform skillfully	Observe, focus attention, listen, perform, do, question, conduct, work, read, speak, assemble, operate, use, demonstrate, measure, investigate, model, collect, dramatize	Read fluently Oral presentations Play an instrument Use laboratory equipment Conduct investigations

Table 4-1   **Types of Achievement Targets—Key Words** *(continued)*

Target Type	Explanation	Content Standards/ Benchmark Key Words	Examples
Products	Where the characteristics of the final product are important; using one's knowledge, reasoning, and skills to produce a final product	Design, produce, create, develop, make, write, draw, represent, display, model, construct	Writing Artistic products Research reports Make a map Personal fitness plan Make a model that represents a scientific principle

Source: Adapted from *Classroom Assessment* for *Student Learning: Doing It Right—Using It Well* (p. 64), by R. J. Stiggins, J. Arter, J. Chappuis, & S. Chappuis, 2006, Portland, OR: Assessment Training Institute. Copyright © 2006, 2004 by Educational Testing Service. Adapted by permission.

For example, you might decide that "Knows the binomial theorem" is a reasoning target. Therefore it has knowledge underpinnings—knows what the binomial theorem is and when to use it. It also has reasoning underpinnings that need to be practiced—use the binomial theorem to solve problems, identify problems best solved using it, and so on. All of these things should be incorporated into instruction.

Key Points to Remember

1. Not all benchmarks embody all types of learning targets. There is a hierarchy. Knowledge targets embody no reasoning, skill, or product underpinnings. Reasoning targets require knowledge but no skills or products. Skills targets require underlying knowledge and reasoning, but not products. Product targets might be underpinned by all four types of learning targets.

2. You are looking at what the benchmark requires students to know and be able to do, not how you will assess it. Because the import of this statement might not be immediately obvious, consider "Compare and contrast democracies with other forms of government." This is a reasoning target. It requires the following:

    *   Knowledge of what a democracy is and knowledge of other types of government—purposes and how power is acquired, used, and justified; and how government can affect people.

    *   It also requires practice in comparing and contrasting—a reasoning target— using the knowledge of different forms of government.

You might assess these knowledge and reasoning underpinnings through an oral presentation (a skill). If you unpack the assessment, you get the following underpinnings:

- As stated, the assessment requires knowledge of what a democracy is and knowledge of other types of government—purposes and how power is acquired, used, and justified; and how government can affect people.

- The assessment also requires knowledge of oral presentations, for example, the need to use language that fits the audience, have eye contact, organize the presentation in a way that the audience will understand (and the various options for this), etc.

- As stated, the assessment also requires practice in comparing and contrasting— a reasoning target—using the knowledge of different forms of government.

- But, other reasoning proficiencies are involved in the assessment that are not required by the original standard; for example, choosing one's particular presentation style, organization, and props from all those possible, to serve the needs of the current presentation.

- There are also skills involved in the assessment that are not required by the standard itself: actually giving the oral presentation—modulating voice tone and speed, actually looking at the audience, actually manipulating props, etc.

To summarize: an assessment developed to elicit the desired standards might require other knowledge, reasoning, skills, and/or products that are not actually part of the standard(s) being assessed. So, when you unpack a standard, you might be tempted to list all these. But don't. All of this extra information is not required for the benchmark, just for the assessment. Any knowledge, reasoning, skill, or product that is required for the assessment that is not required for the standard is a potential source of bias that can distort one's ability to determine student status on the learning target(s) under consideration. The effect of these "extras" needs to be minimized or you won't know how students perform on the actual benchmarks under consideration.

Examples

"Drive with skill." This is a skill level target. Therefore, it has only knowledge, reasoning, and skill underpinnings.

Learning to Drive a Car

Knowledge/ Understanding	Know the law
	Understand informal rules of the road, e.g., courtesy
	Understand what different parts of the car do
	Read signs and understand what they mean
	Understand what "creating a danger" means
	Understand what "creating a hazard" means
Reasoning	Analyze road conditions, vehicle performance, and other driver's actions, compare/contrast this information with knowledge and past experience, synthesize information, and evaluate options to make decisions on what to do next.
	Evaluate "am I safe" and synthesize information to take action if needed.
Skills	Steering, shifting, parallel parking, looking, signaling, backing up, etc.
	Fluidity/automaticity in performing driving actions
Products	None (undamaged car . . . ?)

"Distinguish fact from judgment and opinion; recognize stereotypes; compare and contrast historical information." This is a reasoning level target. Therefore, it has only reasoning and knowledge underpinnings.

History Example

Knowledge/ Understanding	What facts are and how to identify them
	What opinions are and how to identify them
	What stereotypes are and how to identify them
	What it means to compare and contrast things
	The basis (bases) or criteria on which to compare and contrast (events, people, conditions, events, consequences?)
Reasoning	Distinguish facts from opinions in the context of news reporting.
	Recognize novel stereotypes.
	Find the correct information on which to compare and contrast.
	Compare and contrast the historical information specified on the bases specified.
Skills	None required
Products	None required

Examples from State Standards

"Students will evaluate different interpretations of historical events."
This is a reasoning level target, therefore it has only knowledge and reasoning underpinnings.

Sample State Standard 1

Knowledge/ Understanding	Students must know and understand key features of each historical event, and must understand each of the alternative interpretations to be evaluated. The teacher must determine if students are to know those things outright or if they can use reference materials to retrieve the required knowledge.
Reasoning	Evaluative reasoning requires judgment about the quality of each interpretation. Thus students must demonstrate both an understanding of the criteria by which one judges the quality of an interpretation and the ability to apply these criteria.
Skills	None required
Products	None required

"Students will use styles appropriate for their audience and purpose, including proper use of voice, word choice, and sentence fluency."
Writing is a product level target, therefore it will have all four types of target underpinnings.

Sample State Standard 2

Knowledge/ Understanding	Writers must possess appropriate understanding of the concept of style as evidenced in voice, word choice, and sentence fluency. They need to know what voice, word choice, and sentence fluency are, why they are important, and the ways they can vary. They need to understand various audiences and purposes for text and how these might influence style. In addition, students must possess knowledge of the topic they are to write about.
Reasoning	Writers must be able to reason through voice, word choice, and sentence fluency choices for novel audiences and purposes. They also must figure out how to make appropriate voice, word choice, and sentence construction decisions while composing original text for various audiences and purposes.
Skills	Students will either write longhand or will compose text on a keyboard. Each requires its own kind of skill competence.
Products	The final evidence of competence will be written products that present evidence of the ability to write effectively for different audiences and purposes.

Directions:

Listed here are several more state benchmarks. Pick one where it is not immediately clear what you would teach, or for which teachers might disagree. Determine the type of target each ultimately represents. Then analyze it for the knowledge/ understanding, reasoning, skill, and/or product prerequisites (as appropriate; remember the hierarchy) needed to perform well on the benchmark. Ask yourself, "What would students need to know and understand to perform well? What reasoning, if any, does this standard require? What skills, if any, would the students need to practice? What products, if any, would students need practice producing?" Practice deconstructing as many as you need to understand the curriculum development task at hand.

1. **Reading, Comprehension Processes, Grades 2–3**—Relate critical facts and details in narrative or information text to comprehend text.

2. **Reading, Comprehension Processes, Grades 6–8**—Interpret text(s) from multiple perspectives (e.g., historical, cultural, gender, political).

3. **Writing, Rhetoric, Grades 4–5**—Convey meaning, provide important information, make a point, fulfill a purpose.

4. **Writing, Rhetoric, Grades 9–12**—Have an organizing structure that gives the writing coherence (e.g., weaves the threads of meaning into a whole).

5. **Social Studies, Political Science/Civics, Grades K–3**—Create and use surveys, interviews, polls, and/or tallies to find information to solve a real problem or make a decision, e.g., create tally sheets to monitor frequency and amount of littering.

6. **Social Studies, Political Science/Civics, Grades 6–8**—Explain and apply tools and methods drawn from political science to examine political issues and/or problems.

7. **Science, Domain I, Inquiry, Grades 4–5**—Design and conduct simple investigations to answer questions or to test ideas about the environment.

8. **Science, Domain I, Inquiry, Grades 9–12**—Communicate and defend scientific explanations and conclusions.

9. **Science, Domain II, Grades K–3**—Explain how sanitary practices, vaccinations, medicines, and other scientific treatments keep people healthy.

10. **Science, Domain II, Grades 6–8**—Describe and exemplify how information and communication technologies affect research and work done in the field of science.

11. **World Languages, Cultures, Grades 4–5**—Identify and use appropriate gestures and other forms of nonverbal communication.

12. **World Languages, Comparisons, Grades 9–12**—Use knowledge of contrasting structural patterns between the target language and the student's own language to communicate effectively.

13. **Music, Singing, Grades K–3**—Sing expressively with appropriate dynamics and phrasing.

14. **Music, Singing, Grades 6–8**—Sing expressively with appropriate dynamics, breath control, phrasing, and nuance, demonstrating understanding of text and style.

Ultimate type of target: 1 = reasoning; 2 = reasoning; 3 = product; 4 = product; 5 = reasoning and product; 6 = knowledge and reasoning; 7 = reasoning and skill; 8 = reasoning and skill or product; 9 = knowledge; 10 = knowledge; 11 = knowledge and skill; 12 = knowledge and reasoning; 13 = skill; 14 = skill.

Competency 3

The leader understands the standards of quality for student assessments, helps teachers learn to assess accurately, and ensures that these standards are met in all school/district assessments.

Have you ever had a parent or student complain about the items or tasks on a teacher's test, citing them as unfair, off target, or confusing? Part of the teacher's professional competence should include knowing how to apply standards of quality to classroom assessment development or selection. Part of the school leader's responsibility is to be able to judge whether a given assessment adheres to these standards. Even though most teachers lack training in classroom assessment, they still develop a majority of their own assessments. Further, selecting ready-made assessments these days is easier than picking questions from the back of the textbook or from other supplementary material. Websites on the Internet and supplemental materials offer test items and tasks to teachers in many subjects in many grade levels, and test item banks remain popular purchases for teacher test construction.

School leaders can evaluate any assessment developed or selected by teachers according to the five Keys to Assessment Quality, discussed in Parts 2 and 3 of this guide. Figure 4-2 serves as a visual reminder of these Keys.

Too often the assessment job of classroom teachers has been removed from their hands. In place of helping teachers become assessment literate, schools and districts may substitute ready-made assessments narrowly designed to prepare for state tests or to generate additional assessment of learning data.

Classroom assessment is not about teachers creating or using mini-versions of the state test. And even though they may be used well in formative ways, it also isn't about conducting short-cycle or common assessments that may or may not adhere to standards of design quality. Classroom assessment is about giving students accurate information about their own learning. When that happens, it enables students to reach the standard on a state test because the scaffolding of learning has been in place in classroom instruction and assessment. The classroom assessment process has helped prepare them with the knowledge and skills necessary to demonstrate that mastery on that test.

A district's development and use of interim/benchmark or common assessments also should adhere to standards of quality. Students who experience success in everyday classroom and interim/benchmark assessment enter into state testing with a higher degree of confidence that they will do well. Large-scale assessments also must adhere to standards of quality if they are to be accurate and reliable. Items of poor quality and

Figure 4-2   **Keys to Quality Classroom Assessment**

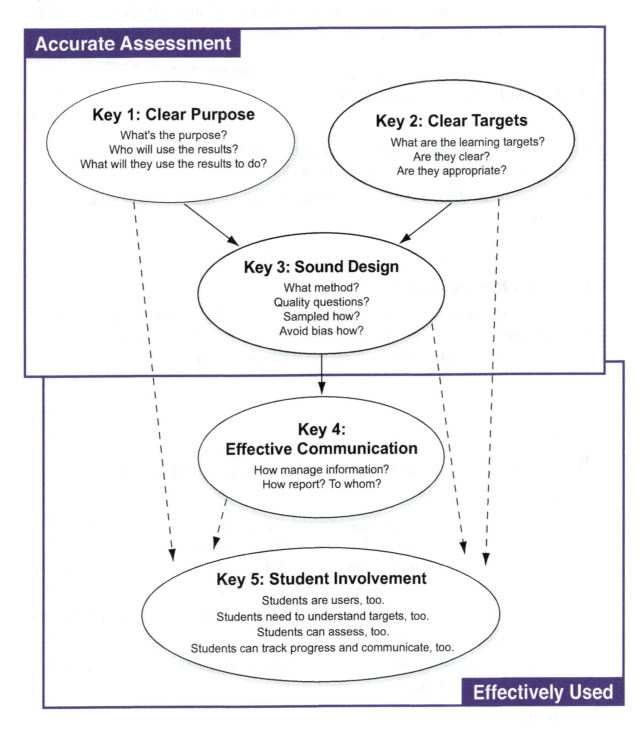

errors in scoring procedures on state tests are common reports in the media and raise public concern about test quality and the credibility of scores. All assessments along this path, formative and summative, need to reflect standards of quality.

Success Indicators for Competency 3

The leader

- Describes the five keys to quality assessment, how they relate to one another, and why they should underpin assessments at all levels.

- Asks questions about data sources to help determine if issues of quality were addressed.

Practice with Competency 3

Identify a classroom teacher who is willing to review and discuss some of her or his classroom assessments. Using the indicators in Table 4-2, discuss with the teacher each one in turn and how they relate to the assessments being reviewed.

Thinking About Assessment
Activity 11: Indicators of Sound Classroom Assessment Practice

Purpose:

Table 4-2 presents a set of indicators of teacher competence for each of the Five Keys to Quality Classroom Assessment: Clear and Appropriate Purposes, Clear and Appropriate Targets, Sound Design, Effective Communication, and Student Involvement. The indicators can be used in at least two ways:

1. Leaders can use them as a basis for discussing with teachers their understanding and use of quality classroom assessments.

2. Teachers can use them to self-assess their own understanding of quality standards for assessment.

Time:

One hour for the main activity

Materials Needed:
- Flipcharts, markers, and easels if available
- Interactive whiteboard or computer with projection if available to assist with recording and viewing work
- Copies of the list of indicators (Table 4-2)

Suggested Room Setup:
- Tables and chairs for small groups to work together
- Space to post the charts around the room for a gallery walk

Directions:

Read through the indicators (Table 4-2). Then divide into pairs or small groups and assign each group one of the Five Keys to Quality Classroom Assessment. Each group brainstorms what strong and weak classroom performance would look like for each indicator and writes them on chart paper. Groups then do a gallery tour— post the charts around the room and everyone walks around, reading each group's responses. Finally, the whole group discusses how you might use the keys, indicators, and performance continua to promote teacher development in this arena.

Table 4-2 **Indicators of Sound Classroom Assessment Practice***

1. Why Assess? Assessment Processes and Results Serve Clear and Appropriate Purposes	a. Teachers understand who and what the users and uses of classroom assessment information are and know their information needs. b. Teachers understand the relationship between assessment and student motivation and craft assessment experiences to maximize motivation. c. Teachers use classroom assessment processes and results formatively (assessment *for* learning). d. Teachers use classroom assessment results summatively (assessment *of* learning) to inform someone beyond the classroom about students' achievement as of a particular point in time. e. Teachers have a comprehensive plan over time for integrating assessment *for* and *of* learning in the classroom.
2. Assess What? Assessments Reflect Clear and Valued Student Learning Targets	a. Teachers have clear learning targets for students; they know how to turn broad statements of content standards into classroom-level targets. b. Teachers understand the various types of learning targets they hold for students. c. Teachers select learning targets focused on the most important things students need to know and be able to do. d. Teachers have a comprehensive plan over time for assessing learning targets.
3. Assess How? Learning Targets Are Translated into Assessments That Yield Accurate Results	a. Teachers understand what the various assessment methods are. b. Teachers choose assessment methods that match intended learning targets. c. Teachers design assessments that serve intended purposes. d. Teachers sample learning appropriately in their assessments. e. Teachers write assessment questions of all types well. f. Teachers avoid sources of bias that distort results.
4. Communicate How? Assessment Results Are Managed Well and Communicated Effectively	a. Teachers record assessment information accurately, keep it confidential, and appropriately combine and summarize it for reporting (including grades). Such summary accurately reflects current level of student learning. b. Teachers select the best reporting option (grades, narratives, portfolios, conferences) for each context (learning targets and users). c. Teachers interpret and use standardized test results correctly. d. Teachers effectively communicate assessment results to students. e. Teachers effectively communicate assessment results to a variety of audiences outside the classroom, including parents, colleagues, and other stakeholders.
5. Involve Students How? Students Are Involved in Their Own Assessment	a. Teachers make learning targets clear to students. b. Teachers involve students in assessing, tracking, and setting goals for their own learning. c. Teachers involve students in communicating about their own learning.

*Sound classroom assessment practice = Skill in gathering accurate information + effective use of information and procedures

Source: Reprinted from *Classroom Assessment* for *Student Learning: Doing It Right—Using It Well* (p. 27), by R. J. Stiggins, J. Arter, J. Chappuis, & S. Chappuis, 2006, Portland, OR: Assessment Training Institute. Copyright © 2006, 2004 by Educational Testing Service. Reprinted by permission.

Thinking About Assessment

Activity 12: Analyze Assessments for Clear Targets*

Purpose:

One of the first places a classroom assessment's accuracy goes astray is in the match to the intended learning. Creating or selecting a test without having a test plan can result in mismatches between instruction and assessment. The assessment probably will not measure what you intended it to measure, which is known as a validity problem. If you have ever faced an exam yourself that did not match what you thought were the most important aspects of the course you were taking, you know what that feels like from the student's point of view. When teachers make a plan for an assessment, whether they intend to create the assessment or just copy it, they are making the advance decisions about validity—what the test will cover and how much weight each learning target will get. In the following activity, teachers will analyze a test they have given to determine its match to the intended learning targets.

Time:

30–60 minutes

Materials Needed:

- A copy of one of each participating teacher's assessments as described in the following directions

- Copies of the blank test plan (shown here and found on the accompanying CD-ROM)

Suggested Room Setup:

Tables and chairs for small groups (content or grade-level teachers may prefer to work together)

Directions:

Ask teachers to bring a selected response or extended written response test they have given to students in the past, or one they plan to give in the near future. Then have them follow these steps to audit it for clear targets.

---

*This activity is adapted from *Classroom Assessment* for *Student Learning: Doing It Right—Using It Well* (pp.108–109), R.J. Stiggins, J. Arter, J. Chappuis, & S. Chappuis, 2006, Portland, OR: Assessment Training Institute. Copyright © 2006, 2004 by Educational Testing Service. Adapted by permission.

1. *Analyze your test item by item.*

   Identify and write down what learning each item assesses. Describe the learning in whatever terms you want. If two or more items address the same learning, use the same terms to describe that learning.

2. *Organize the learning targets into a test plan.*

   Transfer the information from Step 1 to the blank plan. Use the example that follows as your guide.

Learning Target	Item #s	# of points

Example of Step 2 for an Elementary Math Test

Learning Target	Item #s	# of points
Number Sense: Place value	1, 5, 9, 11, 16	10
Representation	2	4
Number Operations: Fractions, multiply by 2, subtract with borrowing	4, 12	5
Problem Solving/Add with carrying	3	3
Measurement: Identify correct units	7, 10, 14, 15	7
Data Analysis & Probability: Tables, charts, and graphs	13	3
Algebra: number patterns, number sentences	6, 8	4

3. *Question your test plan: Is this a representative sample of what you taught and what you expected students to learn? How does it relate to standards?*

   • Does the number of points for each learning target represent its relative importance within the whole? If not, which ones are out of balance? Are some learning targets overrepresented? If so, which one(s)? Are some learning targets underrepresented? If so, which one(s)?

   • Does the number of points for each learning target represent the amount of time you spent on it relative to the whole? If not, which ones are out of balance?

   • Are some of the important learning targets you taught left out? If so, which one(s)?

   • How does your assessment reflect content standards?

4. *Adjust your test plan.*

   As needed, adjust the numbers in the "# of points" column on the chart in Step 2 to reflect both the amount of time you spent teaching each learning target and each target's relative importance to the content as a whole.

   As needed, add or delete learning targets to reflect what you taught and what you deemed most important to learn and assess.

5. *Draw conclusions about your assessment.*

   What does this tell you about the matches among what's written in your curriculum, what you taught, and what you assessed?

Closure:

Ask teachers to complete this sentence with whatever comes to mind:

Without clear targets . . .

Or, you could use this phrase:

Without knowing what each question on a test measures, we can't . . .

You may wish to have them write their thoughts in one or two minutes, collect them, and read them aloud (using no names) to end the session. Here are some likely (and not so likely, but true) answers:

Without clear targets, or without knowing what each question on a test measures, we can't . . .

- Know if the assessment adequately covers and samples what we taught.
- Correctly identify what students know and don't know and their level of achievement.
- Plan the next steps in instruction.
- Give detailed, descriptive feedback to students.
- Have students self-assess or set goals likely to help them learn more.
- Keep track of student learning target by target or standard by standard.
- Complete a standards-based report card.

Competency 4

The leader knows assessment for learning practices and works with staff to integrate them into classroom instruction.

Over the years educators have been encouraged to think about assessment and instruction as hand-in-glove, to think about teaching as one seamless act melding curriculum, instruction, and assessment. In Part 3 we described seven strategies of assessment *for* learning (Chappuis, 2009). These strategies are our best answer to teachers' frequently asked question, "Exactly how do I integrate assessment with instruction and truly make one an extension of the other?" The application of the seven strategies achieves just that in the classroom, with assessment becoming another form of good teaching.

Assessment *for* learning comes during learning, not at the end. Its aim is less to measure learning than to promote it, and goes beyond traditional formative assessment in that students play an active role in using the assessment process and its results to manage and plan their own learning. Here are some examples of what assessment-literate teachers do when applying the seven strategies of assessment *for* learning:

- Teachers understand and can articulate *in advance of teaching* the achievement targets students are to hit.

- *Students are informed regularly* about those targets in terms they can understand, in part through the study of the criteria by which their work will be evaluated, and samples of high-quality work. As a result, *students can describe what targets they are to hit* and what comes next in their learning.

- Both the teacher and the student use classroom assessment information to *revise and guide* teaching and learning.

- Teach students the skills of self-assessment.

- Provide students descriptive feedback linked directly to the intended learning targets, giving them insight about current strengths and how to do better next time, rather than giving evaluative feedback consisting only of marks and letter grades. Students have an opportunity to practice, using this feedback, before a summative assessment.

- Keep students connected to a vision of quality as the learning unfolds, continually defining for students what the learning expectations are for the lesson/unit. Involve students in their own assessment in ways that require them to think about their own progress, communicate their own understanding of what they have learned, and set goals to close the gap between where they are now relative to the intended learning and where they need to be to meet standards.

- Assessment-literate teachers teach students how to present their work/progress in conferences, have students create practice test items, and evaluate anonymous classroom work for quality—all examples of students being involved in assessment.

- Have students communicate the status of their own learning to interested adults through written journals, student-involved parent conferences, and portfolios that focus on growth toward the standards.

Success Indicators for Competency 4

The leader

- Can differentiate between assessment *of* and *for* learning and can explain specific classroom assessment *for* learning practices.

- Can provide examples of what assessment *for* learning looks like in the classroom, including how students might be involved.

Practice with Competency 4

Differentiate between assessment *of* and *for* learning for a colleague or on paper. Include their relationship and the differences between the two.

Write in your own words the seven strategies of assessment *for* learning and a statement of rationale for their use in the classroom. In commonsense terms, what would appear to be the benefits for students of the use of each strategy in the classroom?

Thinking About Assessment

Activity 13: Communicating Learning Targets in Student-friendly Language

Purpose:

This activity is designed for use with a group of teachers to introduce and practice the process of converting a reasoning learning target into student-friendly language.

Time:

45–60 minutes (Can be broken into two parts, with the second part beginning at Step 5)

Materials Needed:

The handout "Converting Learning Targets to Student-friendly Language" (shown here and found on the accompanying CD-ROM); participants can also bring their content standards for one subject or class

Suggested Room Setup:

Tables and chairs arranged so that teachers can work in job-alike groups

Context:

The process of making learning targets clear to students can take many forms, which are explained fully in Chapter 2 of *Seven Strategies of Assessment* for *Learning* (Chappuis, 2009). This activity is useful when you want teachers to understand one way to help students answer the assessment *for* learning question "Where am I going?" by defining key terms in a content standard or learning target.

Caution:

The process is not a one-size-fits-all remedy for making targets clear to students. It is especially suited to the patterns of reasoning represented in each subject's content standards. More complex learning targets may require a rubric to fully define them as well as a process for converting the rubric into student-friendly language, which can be accomplished as a part of a learning team's work as they study one of the assessment texts explaining this (Arter & Chappuis, 2006, Chapter 3; Chappuis, 2009, Chapter 2; Stiggins et al., 2006, Chapter 7).

Directions:

1. Briefly describe the rationale for making learning targets clear to students. Explain that this activity shows one way to do that and that it is especially suited to learning targets that require students to reason.

2. Distribute the handout and explain the process, showing how it would work for the learning target "Summarize text."

3. Then ask teachers to select either "Infer" or "Hypothesize" and working with a partner, define the word and then translate it into language that their students would understand.

4. Ask volunteers to share both their definition and the student-friendly language. After hearing several examples, ask table groups to select one and come to consensus on both the definition and student-friendly language for it. Have tables share the consensus language.

5. Ask teachers to work with their subject-area colleagues (at the elementary level, ask teachers to select a subject area by grade level) to identify a content standard from their own curriculum that would benefit from this process. Have them use the process to create a definition of words needing defining and then to write the learning target in student-friendly language.

6. Ask volunteers to share the original learning target and their student-friendly version.

7. As closure you may wish to ask teachers to use the student-friendly versions they have created with students and come back together after a short time to discuss what they did with the targets and what they noticed happening with students as a result.

Converting Learning Targets to Student-friendly Language

Select a learning target that would be made clearer by this process. Reasoning learning targets are often good candidates. Then use the following process to convert it into student-friendly language.

The Process

1. Identify the word(s) and/or phrase(s) needing clarification. Which terms will students struggle with? Imagine stating the target in its original form to your class. Then envision the degree of understanding reflected on faces throughout the room. At which word did they lose meaning?

2. Define the term(s) you have identified. Use a dictionary, your textbook, your state content standards document, or other reference materials specific to your subject. If you are working with a colleague, come to agreement on definitions.

3. Convert the definition(s) into language your students are likely to understand.

4. Turn the student-friendly definition into an "I" or a "We" statement: "I can _____"; "I am learning to _____"; or "We are learning to _____." Run it by a colleague for feedback.

5. Try the definition out with students. Note their responses. Refine as needed.

6. Let students have a go at this procedure occasionally, using learning targets you think they could successfully define and paraphrase. Make sure the definition they concoct is congruent with your vision of the target.

The Process in Action

> **Learning target:** Summarize text.
>
> **Word to be defined:** *Summarize*
>
> **Definition:** to give a brief statement of the main ideas and significant details
>
> **Student-friendly language:** I can summarize text. This means I can make a short statement of the main ideas and most important details from a passage I have read.
>
>
> **Learning target:** Make predictions.
>
> **Word to be defined:** *Prediction*
>
> **Definition:** A statement saying that something will happen in the future
>
> **Student-friendly language:** I can make predictions. This means I can use information from what I read to guess at what will happen next. (Or, to guess what the author will tell me next.)

Your turn...

> Working with a partner, select either *infer* or *hypothesize* and follow the process to convert it to student-friendly language.
>
> **Word to be defined:** *Infer*
>
> **Definition:**
>
>
> **Student-friendly language:** I can infer. This means I can
>
>
>
> **Word to be defined:** *Hypothesize*
>
> **Definition:**
>
>
>
> **Student-friendly definition:** I can hypothesize. This means I can

Source: Process description reprinted from *Seven Strategies of Assessment* for *Learning* (p. 23), by J. Chappuis, 2009, Portland, OR: ETS Assessment Training Institute. Reprinted with permission.

Thinking About Assessment

Activity 14: Assessment *for* Learning Self-evaluation

Purpose:

To offer teachers an opportunity to think about where they are now with respect to key assessment *for* learning practices.

Time:

25–30 minutes

Materials Needed:

- A copy of the handout "Assessment *for* Learning Self-evaluation" for each participant (shown here and found on the accompanying CD-ROM)

- The numbers 1 through 5 each written on a separate 8 1/2 x 11 piece of paper (for posting on the wall)

- The graphing chart (shown here and found on the accompanying CD-ROM) reproduced as a large poster

- A fat-tip marker (1/2 to 3/4 inch)

Suggested Room Setup:

- Tables for participants' independent work (Direction item 1)

- Open wall space with the numbers 1 through 5 posted about six feet high and three to five feet apart so that people will be able to see them when lined up (Direction items 2 and 3)

Directions:

1. Ask participants to number from 1 through 6 on a separate piece of paper. Tell them not to put their names on it—this activity will be anonymous. Then have them evaluate their own classroom practice for each of the six statements on the survey "Assessment *for* Learning Self-evaluation" using the scale of 1 through 5 as described on the survey. This usually takes about five minutes.

2. After everyone has finished, have participants wad their papers into snowballs, move to the open area, and form a circle. Ask them to throw their snowballs at each other, picking one up and throwing it to someone else two or three times. This usually takes about five minutes.

3. Ask everyone to find a snowball, open the paper up and "be" that person. They should find the rating next to statement 1 (it will be a number from one through five), and line up in front of the appropriate number you have posted on the wall. Ask the person at the head of each line to count the people. Graph the number of people standing in each line on the chart, using a fat marker.

Then read the statement aloud. Do the same for each of the remaining statements. This usually takes about ten minutes.

4. Debrief by asking participants to find a partner and comment on the results they see charted and implications for further learning. Then conduct a large-group discussion of observations. This usually takes five to ten minutes.

Assessment *for* Learning Self-evaluation

On a separate piece of paper, number from 1 through 6.

Rate your current classroom practice for each of the six statements by using the following scale:

1 = I don't do this, or this doesn't happen in my classroom.

2 = I do this infrequently, or this happens infrequently in my classroom.

3 = I do this sometimes, or this sometimes happens in my classroom.

4 = I do this frequently, or this happens frequently in my classroom.

5 = I do this on an on-going basis, or this happens all the time in my classroom.

Survey Statements

1. I communicate learning targets to students in language they can understand, as a regular part of instruction.

2. I use examples and models to help students understand key elements of a quality response, product, or performance.

3. I offer feedback that links directly to the intended learning, pointing out strengths and offering information to guide improvement. Students receive this feedback during the learning process, with opportunities to improve on each learning target before the graded event.

4. I design assignments and assessments so that students can self-assess, by identifying their own strengths and areas for further study in terms of intended learning. The results of assignments and assessments function as effective feedback to students.

5. I use assessment information to focus instruction day-to-day in the classroom.

6. I give students regular opportunities to track, reflect on, and share their achievement status and improvement.

Assessment *for* Learning Self-evaluation Results Graph

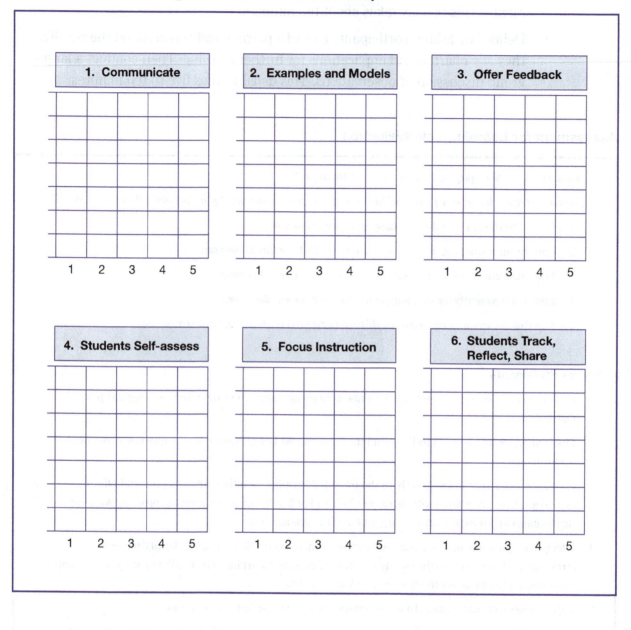

Competency 5

The leader creates the conditions necessary for the appropriate use and reporting of student achievement information, and can communicate effectively with all members of the school community about student assessment results, including report card grades, and their relationship to improving curriculum and instruction.

Because test scores and traditional report card grades do not communicate sufficient detail about student learning to support that learning as it moves forward, educational leaders need to understand the communication options available that can offer that support, including standards-based grading practices and using students as communicators of their own progress toward standards. Communication or feedback to students about their own progress can be delivered in two forms: evaluative or descriptive. As we discussed in Part 3, finished student work receives a score or grade indicating its quality. This score or grade is *evaluative feedback*. During learning students need information focusing on current mastery, what needs work, and how to succeed at reaching the learning targets. This information is

> *Unfortunately, some teachers do not know how or when to give good descriptive feedback, as it has not been part of their training or staff development.*

descriptive feedback. With good descriptive feedback, teachers and parents also know students' strengths and areas for improvement and can use this information to guide them to mastery. Unfortunately, some teachers do not know how or when to give good descriptive feedback, as it has not been part of their training or staff development.

Both evaluative and descriptive feedback are forms of communication, and both must be done accurately and effectively to be useful to their users. Leaders must provide opportunities for teachers to understand both types of feedback, and to learn how to implement both in the classroom and beyond. We detailed the differences in Part 3, Action 5. But there are other communication challenges for leaders. too.

Communicating Annual Test Scores to Parents and Community

One of the most important communication challenges faced by school leaders is the reporting of annual standardized test results. School leaders need to help parents understand these assessments in ways that go beyond the scoreboard presented in the newspapers. Each time a standardized test is administered at school, whether at the department, school, district, or state level, leaders need to communicate with parents/ guardians about the purpose of the assessment. To help parents put assessment in context, school leaders can send a letter home explaining what is being assessed and why, how the results will be used and by whom, and the relationship between the assessment and the improvement of the instructional program at the school (see Activity 17 for practice).

We recommend including the following components in such a communication with parents:

- Explanation of what the tests measure

- How long the test takes, if it is timed (and why or why not)

- What assessment methods are used

- How the test is scored

- Sample test items showing what the test looks like

- Written tutorials on how to interpret the results

- Sample interpretations of the results

- How the results are intended to be used, and how you will use them (linking the uses you will make of the information to the kinds of uses for which the test is designed)

Schools can hold parent meetings to review these topics, as well as where each test fits into the total assessment program and what the results mean for individual students as they progress through the system. This helps create a foundation for common understanding and effective communication between the school and home. Teachers also can help parents use the test information wisely by cautioning them about how too much attention given to any one indicator of student achievement can skew the picture of individual or group progress. When educators clearly communicate the results of standardized testing in relation to state standards, and use report cards that communicate progress toward those same standards, parents get a more complete picture from the school about what students know and can do relative to a predetermined standard (Chappuis & Chappuis, 2002).

Grading and Reporting

If grades are to reflect something meaningful and serve a useful communications function they must be based on accurate assessments. But, grading practices themselves can present many difficult and potentially contentious issues. Unless resolved, these issues can result in inaccurate communication about student learning. The most common grading problems that lead to faulty grades are summarized in O'Connor's (2007) *A Repair Kit for Grading*.

Some software grading programs, while on the surface appearing fair and precise, can use computerized routines to generate grades that are neither fair nor precise (Guskey, 2002). When the report card grade obscures more than it reveals about achievement, school leaders must take action to create the conditions needed to institute clarity and accuracy in both grading and communication about achievement that goes beyond grades.

Schools and districts that have moved or are moving to new reporting systems based on student attainment of content standards can take steps to ensure both students and parents understand how student progress will now be reported, by comparing and contrasting for parents a traditional report card based on A–F letter grades with a new standards-based model, describing the characteristics of and the philosophical foundation for each type of system. Informing students and parents of what is and is not factored into the report card grade also is important in building a common understanding. Also, leaders should ensure their systems use as few coded messages as possible (B–, 79%, satisfactory, emerging), always providing clear definitions of what those symbols mean.

Success Indicators for Competency 5

The leader

- Differentiates between evaluative and descriptive feedback and can explain why it is important to balance them in the classroom.

- Understands the meaning of the various test scores and other forms of evidence of learning available to them and can interpret those scores correctly in terms of the inferences about student achievement each permits.

- Understands the differences between sound and unsound classroom grading practices.

- Sees the connection between standards-based reporting processes and standards-based assessments, and works to develop such a communication system.

Practice with Competency 5

Create a chart that differentiates between evaluative and descriptive feedback, depicting similarities and differences and how teachers can balance the two.

List those items that can be factored into a grade that can misrepresent the level of student achievement.

Prepare a list of tests given in your school or district. See if you can describe the score provided for each in parent-friendly terms, describing the use and potential misuse of the scores.

 Thinking About Assessment

Activity 15: A Rubric for Sound Grading Practice

Purpose:

The rubric that follows supports the three principles for grading we recommend:

— The purpose of grades is to communicate

— Grades should communicate only about student achievement

— Grades should reflect the current level of achievement

The rubric represents our best thinking at the current time on what constitutes sound grading practice—i.e., grading practices that best support classroom assessment both *of* and *for* learning. To understand the rubric fully and use it well, both leaders and teachers need to engage in comprehensive study of sound classroom assessment practices.

Time:

One hour

Materials Needed:

* Copies of the grading rubric for each participant (Table 4-3, shown here and found on the accompanying CD-ROM)
* Copies of school/district grading policies

Suggested Room Setup:

Tables and chairs set up for easy analysis and discussion among participants

Directions:

Use the rubric (Table 4-3) as a discussion starter for both practice and policy. Analyze your staff practices to see how nearly they approach the stated grading guidelines. Analyze your current school/district policies on grading in terms of what is currently in them relative to the rubric and what is missing. What steps would you need to take to align your grading policies and staff practices with these guidelines?

Table 4-3 **Rubric for Sound Grading Practice***

Criterion	Beginning	Developing	Fluent
1. Organizing the gradebook	The evidence of learning (e.g., a gradebook) is entirely organized by sources of information (tests, quizzes, homework, labs, etc.).	The evidence of learning (e.g., a gradebook) is organized by sources of information mixed with specific content standards.	The evidence of learning (e.g., a gradebook) is completely organized by student learning outcomes (content standards, benchmarks, grade level indicators, curriculum expectations)
2. Including factors in the grade	Overall summary grades are based on a mix of achievement and nonachievement factors (e.g., timeliness of work, attitude, effort, cheating). Nonachievement factors have a major impact on grades. Extra credit points are given for extra work completed; without connection to extra learning. Cheating, late work, and missing work result in a zero (or a radically lower score) in the gradebook. There is no opportunity to make up such work, except in a few cases. Borderline-grade cases are handled by considering nonachievement factors.	Overall summary grades are based on a mix of achievement and nonachievement factors, but achievement counts a lot more. Some extra credit points are given for extra work completed; some extra credit work is used to provide extra evidence of student learning. Cheating, late work, and missing work result in a zero (or lower score) in the gradebook. But, there is an opportunity to make up work and replace the zero or raise the lower score. Borderline cases are handled by considering a combination of nonachievement factors and collecting evidence of student learning.	Overall summary grades are based on achievement only. Extra credit work is evaluated for quality and is only used to provide extra evidence of learning. Credit is not awarded merely for completion of work. Cheating, late work, and missing work is recorded as "incomplete" or "not enough information" rather than "0." There is an opportunity to replace an "incomplete" with a score without penalty. Borderline grade cases are handled by collecting additional evidence of student achievement, not by counting nonachievement factors.

*Based on suggestions from Ken O'Connor, personal communication, 2003. Copyright 2005, ATI and Ken O'Connor.

Table 4-3 **Rubric for Sound Grading Practice** *(continued)*

Criterion	Beginning	Developing	Fluent
3. Considering assessment purpose	Everything each student does is given a score and every score goes into the final grade. There is no distinction between "scores" on practice work (formative assessment or many types of homework) and scores on work to demonstrate level of achievement (summative assessment).	Some distinctions are made between formative (practice such as homework) and summative assessment, but practice work still constitutes a significant part of the grade.	Student work is assessed frequently (formative assessment) and graded occasionally (summative assessment). "Scores" on formative assessments and other practice work (e.g., homework) are used descriptively to inform teachers and students of what has been learned and the next steps in learning. Grades are based only on summative assessments.
4. Considering most recent information	All assessment data is cumulative and used in calculating a final summative grade. No consideration is given to identifying or using the most current information.	More current evidence is given consideration at times but does not entirely replace out-of-date evidence.	Most recent evidence completely replaces out-of-date evidence when it is reasonable to do so. For example, how well students write at the end of the grading period is more important than how well they write at the beginning, and later evidence of improved content understanding is more important than early evidence.

Table 4-3   **Rubric for Sound Grading Practice** *(continued)*

Criterion	Beginning	Developing	Fluent
5. Summarizing information and determining final grade	The gradebook has a mixture of ABC, percentages, +✓-, and/or rubric scores, etc. with no explanation of how they are to be combined into a final summary grade. Rubric scores are converted to percentages when averaged with other scores—or—there is no provision for combining rubric & percentage scores. Final summary grades are based on a curve—a student's place in the rank order of student achievement. Final grades for special needs students are not based on learning targets as specified in the IEP. Final summary grades are based on calculation of mean (average) only.	The gradebook may or may not have a mixture of symbols, but there is some attempt, even if incomplete, to explain how to combine them. Rubric scores are not directly converted to percentages; some type of decision rule is used, the final grade many times does not best depict level of student achievement. Final grades are criterion referenced, not norm referenced. They are based on preset standards such as A = 90–100% and B = 80–89%. But, there is no indication of the necessity to ensure shared meaning of symbols—i.e., there is no definition of each standard. There is an attempt to base final grades for special needs students on learning targets in the IEP, but the attempt is not always successful—or—it is not clear to all parties that modified learning targets are used to assign a grade. The teacher understands various measures of central tendency, but may not always choose the best one to accurately describe student achievement.	The gradebook may or may not have a mix of symbol types, but there is a sound explanation of how to combine them. Rubric scores are converted to a final grade using a decision rule that results in an accurate depiction of the level of student attainment of the learning targets. Final grades are criterion referenced, not norm referenced. They are based on preset standards with clear descriptions of what each symbol means. These descriptions go beyond A = 90–100% and B = 80–89%; they describe what A, B, etc. performance looks like. Final grades for special needs students are criterion referenced, and indicate level of attainment of the learning goals as specified in the IEP. The targets on which grades are based are clear to all parties. The teacher understands various measures of central tendency (average, median, mode) and understands when each is the most appropriate one to use to accurately describe student learning.

Table 4-3 **Rubric for Sound Grading Practice** *(continued)*

Criterion	Beginning	Developing	Fluent
6. Verifying assessment quality	There is little evidence of consideration of the accuracy/quality of the individual assessments on which grades are based. Quality standards for classroom assessment are not considered and the teacher has trouble articulating standards for quality. Assessments are rarely modified for special needs students when such modifications would provide much more accurate information about student learning.	The teacher tries to base grades on accurate assessment results only, but may not consciously understand all the features of a sound assessment. Some standards of quality are adhered to in judging the accuracy of the assessment results on which grades are based. The teacher can articulate some of these standards—or—uses standards for quality assessment intuitively, but has trouble articulating why an assessment is sound. Assessments are modified for special needs students, but the procedures used may not result in accurate information and/or match provisions in the IEP.	Grades are based only on accurate assessment results. Questionable results are not included. The teacher can articulate standards of quality, and can show evidence of consideration of these standards in his/her classroom assessments: • clear and appropriate learning targets • clear and appropriate for users and uses • sound assessment design (proper method, quality exercises, sound sampling, minimum bias) • effective communication of results Assessments are modified for special needs students in ways that match instructional modifications described in IEPs. Such modifications result in generating accurate information on student achievement.

Table 4-3   **Rubric for Sound Grading Practice** *(continued)*

Criterion	Beginning	Developing	Fluent
7. Student involvement	Grades are a surprise to students because (a) students don't understand the bases on which grades are determined; (b) students have not been involved in their own assessment (learning targets are not clear to them, and/or they do not self-assess and track progress toward the targets); or (c) teacher feedback is only evaluative (a judgment of level of quality) and includes no descriptive component.	Grades are somewhat of a surprise to students because student-involvement practices and descriptive feedback are too limited to give them insights into the nature of the learning targets being pursued and their own performance.	Grades are not a surprise to students because (a) students understand the basis for the grades received; (b) students have been involved in their own assessment throughout the process (they understand the learning targets they are to hit, self-assess in relation to the targets, track their own progress toward the targets, and/or talk about their progress); and/or (c) teacher communication to students is frequent, descriptive, and focuses on what they have learned as well the next steps in learning. Descriptive feedback is related directly to specific and clear learning targets.

Thinking About Assessment

Activity 16: When Grades Don't Match the State Assessment Results

Purpose:

Often we see students with low report card grades but high standardized test scores, and vice versa. This activity has participants explore reasons why there might be a disconnect between report card grades and state test scores.

Time:

10–20 minutes

Materials Needed:

If available, information showing the relationship/disparity between report card grades and state test results

Suggested Room Setup:

Tables and chairs for ease of discussion/participation

Directions:

Together with your teachers read the scenario and then discuss the following questions.

Scenario: Students consistently get high grades but fail to meet competency on a state test. Or the reverse, students get low grades but demonstrate a high level of competency on the state test.

- Why might the situation be occurring? Consider the extent to which conditions for sound communication are violated.

- Are other standards of quality assessment being violated?

Possible reasons: (1) The state assessment only includes achievement, while grades might include factors other than achievement, such as absences. (2) Class work may cover more than the priorities in the state assessment, so classroom assessments might measure different things than the state assessment. (3) The classroom assessments underpinning the grades aren't accurate. (4) It is unclear how the state performance standard cutoff relates to teachers' grading cutoffs. (5) They were given at different times and might not match with respect to the content students have encountered.

Closure:

Discuss what you can do in your school or district to deal with this situation.

Possible solutions: (1) Clarify state assessment and classroom learning targets. Do they match? If not, should they? Is instruction aligned? (2) Check classroom assessments for accuracy—do they meet the five Keys to Assessment Quality? (3) Calibrate classroom assessments to the state assessment so that teachers and students know the level needed to perform on classroom assessments to meet state standards.

 Thinking About Assessment

Activity 17: A Standard Cover Letter to Parents

Purpose:

Parents report they appreciate proactive efforts on the part of the school to communicate with them about important matters, including school testing. Whenever possible, communicating with parents preceding test administration helps put the test in context and build support for the school assessment program. When not possible or practical, a letter home from the school after the test has been taken is essential. This activity helps schools prepare a cover letter to parents for an upcoming test.

Time:

30–60 minutes

Materials Needed:

- Copies of the assessment audit done in Activity 4
- Materials or equipment for drafting a sample cover letter

Suggested Room Setup:

Tables and chairs for leaders to work in elementary and secondary groups

Directions:

The sample letter that follows is for a norm-referenced test and provides information from the following list. The letter can be adapted for a standards-based or diagnostic assessment, and may include other information specific to that assessment or based on the local interests of parents:

- A brief explanation of the test, including the purpose of the assessment, the grade levels to be taking the test, the amount of time the test will take, etc.
- What learning targets are assessed, and how those targets relate to the total district curriculum
- How the test items are scored
- What assessment methods are used
- How the results will be reported and used
- What strategies parents can use to help students improve
- And for more information, contact . . .

Refer to the assessment audit that you conducted in Activity 4 in Part 3 of this guide. The grids created in that activity could act as the information foundation for any communication that goes home to parents about tests being given at school. As a team determine which assessments need a cover letter to inform parents about these assessments and their uses in addressing student learning.

Date

Dear Parent,

Last May your tenth-grade student took the _____ Test of High School Skills along with all other tenth graders at other high schools in ABC School District. This combination of tests is designed to measure your student's general progress in fundamental high school skills as compared to that of a national comparison group called the "norm" group. It is administered by the district for the purpose of identifying students who are low in skill levels and therefore perhaps not on track to pass the state test administered in the senior year. As you may know, a passing score on that test is required for graduation, and our intent is to identify those students who need additional help in preparing for that test.

The test taken in May had three sections: reading, language use, and mathematics. The items are drawn from a general national curriculum, and are not specifically designed to match the curriculum in either ABC School District or the state of _____. They are traditional multiple-choice tests, and students mark their response to each question on a separate answer document. The answer sheets are then machine scored by _____, the leading test publisher in the country. The results arrived in the summer and we are providing them to you now.

Tests of this kind come with many different score reports. But the score to examine most closely is the NPR. It stands for National Percentile Rank and tells you the percent of students in the norm group who scored below that score. So, if your student is at the 50th NPR, it means that 50 percent of the students in the norm group had fewer items correct than your child. The 50th percentile is the score that would be earned by a typical tenth grader. Because test scores of this type are not always exact indicators of a student's skill level, the district will consider other information, including other test scores, student GPAs, and individual teacher comments and observations before determining which students will be offered additional assistance.

Additionally, these test results will be used to examine strengths and weaknesses in our district curriculum and instructional practices. If you have any questions, please contact the _____ at _____.

Sincerely,

Principal
or
Assistant Superintendent for Curriculum

Competency 6

The leader understands the issues related to the unethical and inappropriate use of student assessment and protects students and staff from such misuse.

School leaders are responsible for protecting the well-being of students whose achievement is assessed either by means of standardized tests or through classroom assessment. This standard is met when leaders promote interpretation, use, and communication of results that lead to appropriate inferences about student learning and proper action on behalf of student success. Leaders are obliged in all contexts to help avoid and discourage misinterpretation, misuse, and miscommunication of assessment results.

School leaders also have a responsibility to protect the confidentiality of individual student assessment results, obtain parental consent for certain assessments prior to the assessment being given, and follow procedures that protect test security. They also need to ensure that students with special needs be provided with assessment accommodations appropriate for their circumstance and consistent with their own IEP (OSPI, 1996; Stiggins, 2008). Allowing the widest range of students possible to participate in school testing programs provides the most accurate picture of system performance, and gives as many students as possible the opportunity to show what they know.

Monitoring test preparation practices is another important part of the leader's ethical responsibilities. The best test preparation comes from a high-quality curriculum and good teaching, but there is a great deal of pressure today to raise test scores, so it becomes paramount that educators understand the differences between ethical and unethical practices. Ethical practices are aimed at raising student achievement; some unethical practices bypass fostering genuine learning and go directly to raising test scores.

Some state tests measure a narrow slice of their state content standards; by assessing only what is easily measured, the tests do not address many important content standards (Commission on Instructionally Supportive Assessment, 2001). In such cases, school leaders need to guard against the practice of narrowing the curriculum to teach only to those standards easily tested at the state level. This can skew the curriculum balance in favor of learning at the knowledge level, at the expense of how to reason, perform skillfully with that knowledge, and create quality products (Chappuis & Chappuis, 2002).

This is not in conflict with the practice of some districts, where they identify "power" or "essential" standards. As long as these standards are balanced across types of learning targets and reflect the most important objectives for students to master, not just the tested ones, this practice can contribute to focusing instruction on standards. To deepen your understanding of issues related to ethical and appropriate use of student assessment in all forms we recommend that you review the following resources:

- *Code of Fair Testing Practices in Education,* Joint Committee on Testing Practices (Washington, DC: Author, 2003). Mailing Address: Joint Committee on Testing Practices, Science Directorate, American Psychological Association, 750 First Street, NE, Washington, DC 20002-4242. This is a collaborative publication of the American Counseling Association, American Educational Research Association, American Psychological Association, American Speech-Language-Hearing Association, American Association of School Psychologists, National Association of Test Directors, and National Council on Measurement in Education. Available online at www.ncme.org under "Publications" and as a PDF download at http://www.apa.org/science/FinalCode.pdf.

- *The Student Evaluation Standards: How to Improve Evaluation of Students,* Joint Committee on Standards for Educational Evaluation (Thousand Oaks, CA: Corwin, 2004). This is a joint publication of Corwin Press and Educational Testing Service Educational Policy Leadership Institute, Princeton, NJ.

Success Indicators for Competency 6

The leader

- Understands and values a set of moral principles related to the assessment of student learning and the appropriate communication and use of results.

- Knows how to select or develop assessments that meet accepted standards of assessment quality.

- Knows how to administer assessments in a manner that ensures all students an equal opportunity to demonstrate competence.

- Knows how to report results to ensure users' understanding.

Practice with Competency 6

Check your district policy handbook or school faculty handbook. What is said about ethical test preparation? Should new wording be considered?

What are the most common forms of test accommodations you are familiar with? Are there others that may also need consideration for use in your school or district?

Thinking About Assessment

Activity 18: "Is This Responsible?"

Purpose:

This activity is for use with a school or district staff to stimulate thinking and discussion about responsible practices before, during, and after standardized testing. We recommend that you use this list as a springboard for your own needs; consider modifying it so that it reflects the kinds of tests your teachers administer and includes those practices you want to discuss with them.

Time:

30–60 minutes

Materials Needed:

Copies of the table "Is This Responsible?" on pp. 155–156 (also found on the accompanying CD-ROM)

Suggested Room Setup:

Tables and chairs set for easy discussion among small groups or as a whole group

Directions:

Have participants read each practice on the table, "Is This Responsible?" found on pp. 155–156, and mark each as "Responsible," "Irresponsible," or "It Depends." Let participants discuss the reasons for their answers with partners or in small groups. Then conduct a large-group discussion. Identify practices on which the whole group has consensus, then discuss those practices on which there is more than one opinion. Or, you could hand out your answers and have discussion center on clarifying why each practice is either responsible or irresponsible, or conditions that are required to be in place for the practice to be one or the other.

Closure:

Hand out a list of appropriate practices developed for your building or district testing situations.

Is This Responsible?

Practice	Responsible	Irresponsible	It Depends
Tell students what the test results will be used for.			
Use locally developed tests that parallel the content of an upcoming standardized test to help students get ready.			
Define on the test form words in the directions that students don't understand.			

Is This Responsible? *(continued)*

Practice	Responsible	Irresponsible	It Depends
Discuss with students how the test will be administered, in advance of the test.			
Incorporate into the curriculum all subject-area objectives measured by an upcoming test.			
Teach test-taking skills.			
Use published test preparation material that promises to raise scores on a specific standardized test.			
During the test, pronounce words used in the test.			
Review skills, strategies, and concepts previously taught just before administering a standardized test.			
Limit curriculum and instruction to the skills, strategies, and concepts included on a standardized test.			
Review standardized test question answers after the test.			
Give help to those students who are confused during the standardized test.			
Exclude eligible students from taking the standardized test.			
Reproduce part of the test to help students understand it after they've taken the test.			
Comment on the quality of student work during the test.			
Hint that a student should change an answer.			
Read a part of the standardized test to a student to help him or her understand it better.			
Keep students focused and on task during the test.			
Teach directly to the state standards that are represented on a standardized test.			
Teach students to apply a performance assessment scoring rubric before a high-stakes assessment.			
Change a student's grade based on recent test evidence revealing a higher level of achievement.			
Report invasions of student test score privacy issues.			
Hand score a sample of student standardized test papers to evaluate the accuracy of electronic scoring services.			

Thinking About Assessment

Activity 19: Guidelines for Test Preparation and Administration

Purpose:

This activity will help you analyze current testing practices in your district or school, using lists of actions that principals or teachers can take to enhance the testing atmosphere in schools. The lists are taken by permission from "Ethical Standards on Testing: Test Preparation and Administration," developed by members of the Washington Educational Research Association (WERA) in 1999 and revised in 2001.

Time:

30 minutes to one hour

Materials Needed:

Copies of the following lists or a copy of this guide for each participant

Suggested Room Setup:

Tables and chairs set for ease of discussion among participants

Directions:

Read through each list and determine which practices are already in place in your building or district. Decide which to implement. Additionally, you may want to find similar documents produced by national organizations and by organizations within your state:

American Educational Research Association, American Psychological Association, National Council of Measurement in Education. (1999). *Standards for educational and psychological testing*. Washington, DC: APA.

American Educational Research Association. (2000). *Ethical standards of the American Educational Research Association*. Washington, DC: Author.

National Council of Measurement in Education, Ad hoc Committee on the Development of a Code of Ethics. (1995; revised 2003). *Code of professional responsibilities in educational measurement*. Washington, DC: Author.

Guidelines for Test Preparation and Administration

The Principal's Role

There are a number of things the principal can do to enhance the testing atmosphere in the school:

1. Inform both students and parents about what each test does and does not do, when and how it will be administered, and how the results will be used. Indicate the importance of tests for students, staff, and the school. Stress the importance of school attendance on the scheduled testing dates.

2. Encourage the implementation of appropriate test-wiseness teaching and review. Teaching test-wiseness skills should be independent of subject matter being tested and should include an understanding of test books, use of answer sheets, item response strategies, time management, listening, and following directions.

3. Let parents know about upcoming tests and what they can do to encourage their children's performance.

4. Work with teachers to develop a building testing schedule. Attempt to maximize the efficiency of the building's physical layout and staff resources.

5. Pay careful attention to building schedules during the testing period. Avoid planning assemblies, fire drills, maintenance, etc., during the testing period.

6. Develop a plan to keep tests and answer sheets secure before and after administration, and ensure that all are returned properly.

7. Arrange, where possible, for teachers to have proctoring help in administering tests. Ensure that tests are carried out according to ethical and legal practice.

8. Provide a policy statement or handbook to all involved with test administration spelling out proper and improper testing procedures.

9. Create a process to check out any suspicions or allegations of cheating.

10. Require a detailed written explanation about why a student was not tested or the reason a score was not figured into a school's average.

11. Encourage teachers' participation in district inservice sessions on assessment.

12. Ensure that all students are tested. Review all test accommodations, including exclusion as a last resort, made for students with special needs. Ensure that accommodations and exclusions are consistent with specific testing program guidelines.

13. Ensure that there are no interruptions in classrooms during the testing period, including custodial tasks, intercom calls, delivery of messages, etc.

14. Work with the test coordinator and classroom teachers to schedule and staff makeup days for students who miss parts of the test. This might include bringing in a substitute or finding other ways to use building staff creatively to administer a makeup test in an appropriate setting.

15. Share test results with staff. Neither the testing program nor the results are "owned" by any particular grade. The results are an indication of how well things are going in the school generally. Staff members need to work together to ensure that the testing process is a smooth one. School improvement is a team effort.

Guidelines for Test Preparation and Administration *(continued)*

The Teacher's Role

Students will do their best on tests if they find an encouraging and supportive atmosphere, if they know that they are well prepared, and if they know that they will do well with hard work. To create a situation that will encourage students to do their best, teachers should do the following:

1. Attend inservice workshops on test administration.

2. Develop an assessment calendar and schedule.

3. Prepare students well in advance for assessment by teaching test-wiseness skills. Independent of subject matter being tested, teach and review test-taking skills that include an understanding of test books and use of answer sheets, item response strategies, time management, listening, and following directions.

4. Develop a list of which and how many students will be tested, and when they will be tested. Determine students for whom special-needs accommodations may be necessary.

5. Develop a list of students who will be exempted from testing and the reason for the exemption. The list must be reviewed and approved by the principal or test administration committee. Parents must be notified and alternative assessments identified.

6. Develop plans for the administration of makeup tests for students absent from the scheduled testing period.

7. Prepare and motivate students just before the test.

8. Prepare to administer the test, with sufficient materials available for all students to be tested.

9. Prepare classrooms for the test. Arrange for comfortable seating where students will not be able to see each others' test materials, but will be able to hear test directions. Eliminate posters or other materials that may be distracting or contain information that could be used with the test.

10. Alert neighboring teachers to the testing schedule and ask their help in keeping noise levels to a minimum.

11. Arrange a separate, supervised area for those students who finish early and may cause a distraction for other students.

12. Read the test administration manual carefully, in advance. Administer the test according to the directions.

13. Meet with proctors to discuss their duties and responsibilities. Carefully and actively proctor the test.

14. Arrange for appropriate breaks and student stress-relievers.

15. Follow the rules for test security and return all test material to the test administrator.

Competency 7

The leader can plan, present, and/or secure professional development activities that contribute to the use of sound assessment practices.

Of the Seven Actions discussed in Part 3 of this guide, each of the first six is an element of Action 7, Promote the Development of Assessment Literacy. Without the knowledge and skills of assessment literacy educators would not balance assessment, ensure classroom assessment quality, turn learners into assessors, provide descriptive feedback, or build the confidence of all learners. Assessment literacy is not hard learning, but it is slow learning and it requires sustained and targeted support. This competency links the school or district's staff development program with the goal of every instructional staff member becoming assessment literate. For example, a principal who wants to establish common quality standards for all end-of-course tests in every subject area must secure the professional development necessary to ensure teachers have the ability to create tests that meet those standards.

To be effective, professional development needs to tend to both the content (what is to be learned) and process (how). Two common professional development models are learning teams and workshops. The learning team model combines research-based assessment content with an adult learning process that honors teacher professionalism, fosters collaboration, and takes place over time, allowing for focus and concentrated effort.

Assessment literacy is not hard learning, but it is slow learning and it requires sustained and targeted support.

The workshop model might instill interest and short-term excitement about new information, but for most individuals it will not be sufficient to change practice long term. Teachers need to deepen their understanding of new practices, try the strategies out in the classroom, and receive feedback on the results. We provide a bit more depth on this topic in a brief article that is part of Activity 20.

Professional development in classroom assessment often connects to professional development in other school/district initiatives and priorities. Finding and establishing those connections and helping teachers see the relationships among them brings coherence to a professional development program that often appears as isolated events entirely disconnected from each other (see Activity 20). For example, when teachers become assessment literate they learn to do assessment planning with the established learning targets. As a result, training in classroom assessment can also be a strategy to assist in implementing the written curriculum. And as leaders help teachers understand and teach the content standards of a given discipline, helping them understand the seven strategies of assessment *for* learning at the same time introduces assessment not just as a vehicle to collect reliable evidence of student learning but also as a form of good instruction.

We all want our professional development programs to, in the end, demonstrably raise student achievement. Evaluating programs for their effectiveness also becomes a leader's responsibility. We address this in more detail in Part 5 of this Action Guide.

Success Indicators for Competency 7

The leader

- Understands the conditions for effective adult learning in schools that improve instruction and student learning.

- Knows that professional development that works calls for a long-term *process* that teaches new ideas and strategies through hands-on practice, coaching, and collaboration.

- Provides leadership support for professional development by ensuring sufficient resources (time and materials) for adult learning and promoting support for ongoing improvement.

Practice with Competency 7

Think about what staff in your building/district know and do right now relative to quality assessment practices. What's missing? What might be the most logical starting place to fill in the gaps?

Draft a school-level professional development plan in classroom assessment, detailing guiding principles, what is to be learned, the learning processes to be used, and how the context will be managed in ways that promote success for all faculty members.

Thinking About Assessment

Activity 20: Supporting Teacher Learning Teams

Purpose:

This activity is designed to engage building and district leaders in a discussion of (1) the rationale for learning teams as a professional development model and (2) the conditions necessary for their success.

Time:

60–90 minutes

Materials Needed:

- A copy of the article, "Supporting Teacher Learning Teams," (presented here and found on the accompanying CD-ROM) for each participant, either distributed in advance or during the session

- Copies for each participant of the six blank "Success Factor" tables shown here (also found on the accompanying CD-ROM)

- Chart paper and markers

Suggested Room Setup:

Tables and chairs set for ease of discussion among participants

Directions:

1. Distribute the article, either during the meeting time or in advance. (If participants are to read it during the meeting, allow an additional fifteen minutes.)

2. Ask participants to discuss their thoughts about the following questions in small groups and then open the discussion up to the large group. You can distribute the questions along with the article if participants are reading in advance of the meeting.

   - What content might the workshop approach to professional development be suited to? Why is the workshop approach not sufficient for developing assessment literacy?

   - In this professional development model, participants are asked to do some independent work—reading a portion of a text, shaping ideas into classroom practice, and then trying them out in the classroom. Why does developing assessment literacy rely on independent work as well as collaborative work? Why must participants' learning responsibility extend beyond attending team meetings?

3. Ask participants to discuss their thoughts about the extent to which the six "success factors" described in the article are present in their organization

(schools or district). Which of these success factors are currently in place? Which will be relatively easy to implement? Which will require significant work to implement? Check the appropriate answer for each factor in the accompanying table. Follow this with a discussion of possible actions to take for each factor.

4. Ask participants to discuss these questions in small groups and then open the discussion up to the large group:

   - Which of the pitfalls described in the article have you already avoided or overcome? How did you do that?

   - Which will need to be addressed?

5. The discussions in this session can contribute to the creation of an action plan to initiate learning-team-based study of *Classroom Assessment* for *Student Learning* (Stiggins et al., 2006) and/or other resources designed to develop teachers' assessment expertise.

SUCCESS FACTOR 1: Create a cultural shift in the school.

Do our teachers understand that acquiring new knowledge and skills is a life-long professional obligation?

Already in place	Will be relatively easy to implement	Will require significant work to implement

Possible actions:

SUCCESS FACTOR 2: Create an understanding of the process.

Do our teachers understand that deepening assessment expertise will involve a commitment to individual as well as collaborative work?

Already in place	Will be relatively easy to implement	Will require significant work to implement

Possible actions:

SUCCESS FACTOR 3: **Address the skills needed for self-directed learning.**

Do our teachers possess the desire and ability to (1) carry out a long-term learning plan systematically, (2) compare their current knowledge and skills with those needed to implement high-quality assessment practices in the classroom, (3) gather evidence of their own learning and progress, and (4) connect their learning to new classroom practices?

Already in place	Will be relatively easy to implement	Will require significant work to implement

Possible actions:

SUCCESS FACTOR 4: **Get the right facilitators.**

Does our school or district have sufficient staff members who possess the skills outlined in the article to facilitate the number of learning teams desired?

Already in place	Will be relatively easy to implement	Will require significant work to implement

Possible actions:

SUCCESS FACTOR 5: **Provide facilitators with adequate support.**

Do we have the capacity to create and maintain a support network for facilitators? Can we add to their knowledge base as needed? Do we have a way to recognize their skills and contributions and to help them communicate the progress of each learning team with principals?

Already in place	Will be relatively easy to implement	Will require significant work to implement

Possible actions:

SUCCESS FACTOR 6: Ensure the active support of school leaders.

Can we as school and district leaders give staff the needed time to develop their assessment skills? Are we able to participate as members of a learning team? Can we articulate the intended learning outcomes of this professional development endeavor? Can we communicate its expected benefits and proven results?

Already in place	Will be relatively easy to implement	Will require significant work to implement
Possible actions:		

Supporting Teacher Learning Teams

Steve Chappuis, Jan Chappuis, and Rick Stiggins

The learning-team model helps teachers make changes in practice that lead to improved student achievement.

Effective professional development is supposed to foster lasting change in the classroom. When it doesn't, we waste valuable time, resources, and most important, our teachers' trust that time engaged in professional development is well spent. We can avoid this by offering proven content in a delivery model that aligns with characteristics of effective adult learning in school. Professional development also works best when it's on-site, job embedded, sustained over time, centered on active learning, and focused on student outcomes (Chappuis, 2007).

We've tried the traditional workshop approach—which typically doesn't incorporate all of these characteristics—to help teachers develop assessment competence. But we've had uneven success, for a variety of reasons. The amount of content to be learned often exceeds what a workshop can cover, even in a series of sessions. A passive "sit 'n' git" mind-set can permeate the environment, even with an engaging presenter and interactive agenda. In addition, there is no opportunity for the presenter to facilitate the reflection, the putting into practice, the collegial discussions, and the learning that can only take place when participants return to their classrooms.

Attending a workshop or conference can help raise awareness of and enthusiasm for a topic, create a shared vocabulary or foundation of knowledge, or act as a catalyst for further learning. However, when the session is over, continuing support for implementation is seldom available. This is a major drawback of the traditional workshop approach.

A More Purposeful Approach

The learning-team model of professional development has gained popularity as schools seek to match the intent of providing deeper, ongoing, teacher-directed learning with the most suitable mode of professional development. Many school districts have altered their calendars and weekly schedules to provide teachers with regular common planning and learning time. Others have incorporated release times for teacher teams during the instructional day. These structural changes provide a foundation for successful adult learning and help remove the barrier of teacher isolation that is, in part, responsible for the lack of effective professional growth (see Fullan as quoted in Sparks, 2003).

However, the learning-team model we recommend involves more than just attending

Source: Reprinted from *Educational Leadership*, Feb. 2009, vol. 66, no. 5, pp. 56–60. Copyright ©2009 ETS Assessment Training Institute. Reprinted with permission.

regular meetings in small groups; it also requires that teachers commit to working and learning *between* team meetings. Change requires individuals to practice with new information and engage in collaborative sharing, a process that presents its own set of challenges.

Ensuring Success

As with other professional development models, adopting and using the learning-team model does not come with an automatic guarantee of success. For every team that succeeds in changing teacher practice, one or more may stall or even fail. To raise the probability that the learning will "take," consider the following recommendations before you implement the learning-team model.

1. Create a cultural shift in the school.

Fullan (in Sparks, 2003) points to cultural barriers, in addition to existing structural barriers, that schools need to overcome to support good professional development. School leaders might begin by stressing the importance of "teachers as learners," helping teachers understand that improving practice by acquiring new knowledge and skills is a professional obligation and that the work of becoming a great teacher is a career-long endeavor. Incentives, such as a stipend, release time, credit applied toward advancement on the local salary schedule, or college credit, then fall into place as a secondary, rather than a primary, motivator or support.

It's essential to emphasize the long-term, ongoing nature of professional development as opposed to a short-term commercially promised quick fix. Participants need to commit up front to an initiative that may

require more of their time and effort than attending afterschool workshops.

Finally, schools should create (and adhere to) group norms for the learning-team experience, such as "Keep the focus on helping students learn," "Involve everyone and make sure all voices are heard," "Stick to the topic or task during meetings," and "Come prepared to meetings."

2. Create an understanding of the process.

Confusion can arise when teachers are accustomed to a model of professional development in which the presenter has all the responsibility for action and the participants' responsibility is limited to just showing up. Set the stage for a change in the delivery mechanism by helping participants understand that the goal of learning teams is to collaboratively strengthen classroom practices that will strengthen student learning.

Learning in learning teams takes place in four related contexts. It begins with an influx of new ideas—through hearing a presentation by an expert, reading books or articles, or viewing an instructional video or footage of classroom practice. Next, it involves shaping the new ideas into classroom practice. Teachers transfer this information to their own contexts by doing such things as preparing lessons, materials, and activities to use with students. Participants then observe and reflect on the results, asking themselves such questions as, What worked? What is the evidence? What needs fine-tuning? and What do I need to learn more about? Finally, participants meet with others to discuss, problem solve, and create. Teachers share what they learned, what they tried, what they observed, what happened with students, and what they still need to work on.

For example, in their study of classroom assessment, participants may read about how to teach students to give one another descriptive feedback. They could try this strategy in their classrooms and then come together to share the specific adaptations they made and the effects they noticed on student learning. They may then discuss how to fine-tune the process for further use.

3. Address the skills needed for self-directed learning.

Some teachers may need to develop specific skills to fully realize the benefits of collaborative, self-directed professional development. Skills that help maximize this model of adult learning include participants' ability to carry out a long-term learning plan systematically and sequentially, compare their current skills and learning needs with the intended learning, gather evidence of their own learning and progress, and connect their learning to new classroom practices (Knowles, 1990).

To develop skills of self-monitoring, for example, the person in charge of the learning team's course of study might identify a list of artifacts that will provide evidence of participants' learning and its effect on student achievement; prepare a protocol for gathering "before," "during," and "after" evidence; and schedule a sharing session for the last team meeting.

4. Get the right facilitators.

Just as the classroom teacher influences student learning more than any other variable does, the skill of the facilitator is central to the success of the learning team. Although it's not always necessary that learning team facilitators be content experts, they should have several skills and dispositions.

For example, they should be able to facilitate discussions, creating a team environment in which all members feel safe and supported even when they disagree by establishing norms that call for this, modeling appropriate responses, and respectfully enforcing adherence to the norms. They should know how to keep the learning focused on transferring new knowledge into classroom practice by bringing the discussion back to this focus with follow-up questions, such as, What have you tried? and How is it working? They should be able to help team members track their growth and its effect on student achievement by organizing a protocol for selecting and reviewing appropriate artifacts.

Skilled facilitators take on the role of "advanced learner," selecting activities matched to the team's needs and doing the reading and activities in advance of meetings so they can help steer team members through unfamiliar or complex concepts. At the same time, they manage the logistical details behind the learning experience, such as preparing agendas, time lines, meeting logs, and handouts.

5. Provide facilitators with adequate support.

Facilitators need to maintain their knowledge base, level of enthusiasm, and facilitation skills to be effective in their roles. School leaders can provide support by creating a network for facilitators, such as a series of regular meetings during which facilitators function as a learning team themselves, sharing what their teams are doing, planning together for their teams' activities, and exploring topics in which they want greater expertise.

School leaders should provide content mini-lessons as needed to deepen facilitators' understanding of the concepts that learning teams are working on. They should recognize the contributions that facilitators have made to developing teacher expertise through venues of professional recognition available in their district. Principals need to be periodically updated on what facilitators are doing and where they are in the program so each principal can stay current with the progress of staff members and provide support accordingly.

6. Ensure the active support of school leaders.

Principals don't just set the tone and climate of the building—they also influence the overall culture in which everything else operates. They need to hold the time allocated to professional development sacred, protecting it from interference or distraction. To promote a sense of accomplishment, they should help teachers track and evaluate their own growth by inquiring about changes they have implemented in their teaching practices and changes they have noted in their students' motivation and achievement. And they should model for their faculties the process of being a continual learner, by participating either as a member of a building's learning team or as a member of a district leadership learning team.

A professional development program will have a greater probability of success when the learning goals are clear to all at the building and district levels. Facilitators and principals need to be in agreement on learning expectations for the team, and building and district leaders should be able to articulate what teachers will be learning and why they're learning it. In addition, district or building leaders should communicate to all staff members the expected benefits and proven results of the professional development focus of study. With a supportive framework, a coherent curriculum, and a skillful facilitator,

teachers can learn without an expert being physically present in the room with them.

Avoiding the Pitfalls

In after-school workshops, things can go wrong. There can be insufficient handouts, faulty technology, bad lighting, a poor sound system, or a presenter with laryngitis.

Unforeseen problems can also derail learning teams. To reduce the likelihood of problems, start by choosing content that rests on a foundation of research that supports its effect on learning and that translates the research into everyday classroom practice. Look for curriculum materials that are teacher-friendly and suitable for use in a learning-team model of professional development.

Make an inventory of all programs or practices that teachers are being asked to learn, along with the learning goals of each. Is there sufficient time and are there sufficient resources to accomplish everything on the teacher learning plate in one year? This is one of the main reasons for the overuse of the workshop model: It can cover lots of material. But covering does not equal learning, either in the classroom or beyond it. Does your program of professional development include time to learn, time to practice, time to discuss, and time to reflect for the learning goals it addresses? If not, it's best to pare the year's adult learning expectations down to what you can do well—or plan for a multiyear implementation.

Carefully consider the composition of the learning team itself, the number of members it should have, and whether they should be from the same department or grade level. Provide a thorough orientation for participants at the outset, including the rationale and context. Explain why you're studying this topic, what's to be gained when it's transferred to the classroom, how long the program will last, and how it's connected to other school and district initiatives.

Schedule meetings in advance and at times that enable all team members to attend. Dedicate that time to learning and to nothing else. In a recent study of a professional development project in which we were involved, the investigator found that "a lack of sufficient meeting time was the single most common constraint cited by teachers in identifying impediments to the successful function of their teams" (Weinbaum, 2008, p. 26).

When at all possible, work with volunteer participants. Our experience has shown that teams are most effective when participants choose to be part of the team as opposed to being required to be there. This may seem at odds with creating a schoolwide culture of learning or a focus on a particular topic, but the two are not mutually exclusive. School leaders can create buy-in through offering initial presentations or short workshops that introduce the content and the research—an overview of what works, why it works, and how it works—along with an example or two that can be useful in the classroom right away.

Stay with the same professional development focus for multiple years, inviting participation each year. Plan for the implementation to become "viral," building to a critical mass.

Finally, clearly communicate the structure and responsibilities of learning-team participation. What separates the learning-team model from many of its professional development cousins is that learning does not just take place during the team meetings. In schools where teacher teams already meet regularly to review data or discuss or decide on schoolwide issues, this will help minimize confusion between those types of team meetings, which tackle a specific issue, and the learning-team professional development meetings, which are better suited to the deeper learning that substantive change requires.

The Best Kind of Learning

Collaborative learning teams provide more than one-time exposure to new ideas. Over time, they can change day-to-day teaching by giving teachers the ongoing opportunity to learn together, apply learning to the classroom, and reflect on what works and why. Just as learning improves for students when they have the structured opportunity to reflect on what they know and don't know in relation to the targets of instruction, adult learning also benefits from intentional reflection on classroom practice. Collaborative learning teams can transform the nature of adult interaction and learning in schools by engaging teachers in the same process of continual learning and improvement that we ask our students to strive for in their work.

Thinking About Assessment

Activity 21: Discussing Key Assessment Concepts with Faculty

Purpose:

This activity is designed for use by building-level leaders to engage staff members in brief introductory discussions of three key concepts: student involvement, assessment accuracy, and the learning team professional development model.

Time:

20–30 minutes for each concept

Materials Needed:

A copy of the selected reading for each participant (presented here and found on the accompanying CD-ROM), either distributed in advance or during the session

Suggested Room Setup:

Tables and chairs set for ease of discussion among participants

Context:

This activity includes three readings: "Engaging Students in the Assessment Process"; "Assessment Quality"; and "Developing Assessment Literacy and Competency." These brief pieces have been adapted from a series of readings written by Charles Osborne, Director of Assessment, Burleson (TX) Intermediate School District, for principals in his district to use with staff to engage in conversations about classroom assessment. This district uses the ATI text *Classroom Assessment* for *Student Learning* (Stiggins et al., 2006) with learning teams as the primary professional development model for developing classroom assessment expertise. The readings and discussions are one part of the district's multi-year support for school principals as they build awareness of the need with their faculties. The first two readings introduce ideas taught in *Classroom Assessment* for *Student Learning*. The third selection introduces the learning team approach to developing classroom assessment expertise.

Directions:

1. Each reading is preceded by notes for the discussion leader and followed by one or more discussion questions, labeled "Personal Reflection." You can use one, two, or all three of the readings, depending on the topics you wish to introduce to your staff. You may want to use the discussion questions that follow each reading, and may also want to create one or more that relate the content to your own context.

2. Identify which of the three readings you will use. Copy the text of the reading for participants.

3. Distribute the reading, either at the beginning of the meeting or in advance. (If participants are to read it during the meeting, allow an additional ten minutes.)

4. Ask participants to discuss their thoughts about the content of the reading and their responses to the "Personal Reflection" questions (or your own discussion questions) in small groups and then open the discussion up to the large group.

READING 1: Engaging Students in the Assessment Process

Notes for the Discussion Leader:

This reading briefly describes four sequential avenues for student involvement. As we succeed in getting students actively engaged in the classroom assessment process a different dynamic begins to work. We begin to see not only a balance of assessment *of* and *for* learning, but the assessment activities, with student involvement, actually form a bond with the instructional process and we start see assessment *as* learning. This is when the role of assessment goes beyond the measurement of learning to serve as an instrument of instruction and learning. This is most evident as students are involved in informal classroom assessment activities, which serve not only to inform teacher and students of the learning at a given point in time, but also as tools to enhance student understanding and learning.

This is an aspect of assessment that we will scarcely see until students are actively involved in the classroom assessment process. When this happens, the connection between classroom instruction and classroom assessment takes on a new dimension. At times it will be difficult to draw a clear line defining if an activity is an instructional strategy or an assessment strategy. We will arrive here as we continue to advance in broadening and improving our classroom assessment and increasing students' involvement in the assessment process.

Engaging Students in the Assessment Process

The idea that we need to include and engage students in the assessment process can generate a number of questions and conflicting understandings. Is student involvement in place if you let the students grade their own papers? Does student involvement mean that students write the tests? These are two examples of the misunderstanding that surround this concept of student involvement.

If we are to succeed in transforming from a teaching organization to a learning organization, it becomes essential that learners become actively involved in the assessment process. How can we become a learning organization if learners are not involved in assessment of the learning? How can we ensure that the learner is involved in a way to enhance learning? In this reading we are going to look at the meaning of including and engaging students in the assessment process. We will look at four avenues within the process where student involvement is most important.

Clearly Defined and Understood Learning Targets

The first avenue of student involvement coincides with one of classroom assessment's core competencies: the importance of clearly defined, articulated, and understood learning targets. While a clear learning target is vitally important to high-quality teaching, it is also essential to achieving high-quality learning. When students know and understand the intended learning, their ability to hit that target greatly increases. Developing and writing the targets is the first stage, but the ultimate benefactors of clear targets are the students. A simple method to gauge this is to ask students about the learning targets. Either of the questions "What are you learning?" or "Why are you doing this activity?" should generate a response that includes a description of the learning target.

Student Self-assessment

The second avenue of student involvement lies in students possessing and practicing the skill of self-assessment relative to the demands of the learning target. This is a skill that must be taught. Self-assessment involves far more than "find the ones you got wrong and correct them." It involves students evaluating their work against the clear learning target by using their understanding of that target and the samples of quality and problematic work provided by the teacher. To maximize learning, this self-assessment occurs prior to turning in an assessment, with opportunities to revise their work before it is graded.

Tracking Their Own Progress

The third avenue of student involvement leads to students tracking their progress in learning through record keeping of that progress. In the acquisition of any knowledge or skill there is a learning progression through which learners pass. As they progress upward toward the knowledge and skill demanded by the state standards, the clear learning targets provide the ladder of ascension. Learners should be able to accurately track the progress of their learning, where they currently stand on the ladder, and the next steps in learning to ascend higher. This practice of tracking learning—whether through the use of a portfolio, tracking progress on individual learning targets, or some other method—serves as a powerful motivator to students to continue improving. It allows them to clearly recognize progress and instills a hope and anticipation of further learning and success. Students' anxiety over report cards or surprise at the results is a clear indication that they have not been tracking their learning through the assessment process.

Engaging Students in the Assessment Process *(continued)*

Communicating about Their Learning to Others

The fourth avenue of student involvement involves students clearly and accurately communicating about their learning progress to others. When they understand the learning targets, competently assess their own strengths and areas for improvement, and track their progress toward standards, communication of that progress becomes a powerful tool. Student-led parent conferences serve as a validation of student effort, confirmation of student progress, affirmation of student competence, and motivation for further learning. These conferences can range from total failure and disaster to exhilarating success. Which it will be hinges on whether students engaged in the actions described by the first three avenues. Student-led parent conferences with students who are not actively involved in the assessment process are a waste of time for the teacher, a source of embarrassment for the learner, and a cause of confusion or frustration for the parent. Conversely, a student-led parent conference where the student has been actively involved is a formula for satisfaction for the teacher, pride for the learner, and joy for the parent.

Source: Adapted with permission from Charles Osborne, Burleson Independent School District, Burleson, TX, 2008.

Personal Reflection:

1. Do we have a method in place to determine that students truly clearly understand and can articulate the learning targets they are responsible for mastering?

2. Am I actively cultivating the skills of self-assessment in my students? Where will I start in teaching these skills?

3. Are students able to track their progress toward mastery of the learning targets? Do I have one or more processes in place to help them do that?

4. What opportunities do students currently have to share their progress with others? What might we do to enhance those experiences for teachers, students, and parents?

READING 2: Assessment Accuracy

Notes for the Discussion Leader:

When it comes to classroom assessment, quantity does not guarantee quality. Although more frequent assessment can improve student achievement, frequent administration of inaccurate assessments holds little hope of improving student achievement. It would be somewhat similar to trying to lose weight and stepping on an inaccurate scale every day. And, relying on textbook or other purchased assessments is also no guarantee of quality. This reading introduces the three keys to classroom assessment quality—clear purpose, clear targets, and sound design—

that are crucial to accuracy of results. (The other two keys—effective communication and student involvement—make up the "Effective Use" portion of the keys to assessment quality.)

As we make progress in using classroom assessment *for* learning, we must not assume that we can rely on already-developed assessments to ensure accuracy. For classroom assessment to deliver on the promise of unparalleled improvement in student performance and motivation, each teacher and administrator must invest time to learn how to evaluate assessments for quality.

A personal reflection question for the discussion leader: As an instructional leader can I also serve as the assessment leader? How can I invest in my teachers becoming assessment literate regarding the quality of the assessments used daily? Am I able to review assessments and evaluate their quality?

Assessment Accuracy

Although following the principles and practices of classroom assessment *for* learning is an essential component in the process of improving student performance, the quality of those classroom assessments is not a neutral factor in the equation. If we attempt to practice assessment *for* learning with poor-quality assessments, we weaken our potential impact. Quality trumps quantity in classroom assessments when improving student learning is the primary value.

Assessment Purpose

The first key to accuracy addresses the intended purpose of the assessment. It asks two questions: "Who is going to use this information?" and "How will they use it?" You may be the person using the information and you may be gathering it to determine a grade, diagnose learning levels, monitor progress, audit the curriculum, group students by needs, sort students for intervention, or any of a plethora of other purposes. Additionally, you may want the information to function as feedback to students, guiding their next steps, or you may want students to use the information to self-assess and set goals for further learning. It is important to note that a single assessment may not be capable of serving a multitude of purposes, as the resulting data may be inadequate or even inaccurate for the decisions we attempt to make. If we are going to have a quality assessment, we must first have a clearly defined purpose of that assignment or assessment—we must determine the intended uses of the information and then design or select the instrument so that it is capable of informing those decisions.

Targets to Be Assessed

The second key to accuracy focuses on the learning targets to be assessed. Are they clear? If the learning targets are vague, the quality of the assessment will suffer. Do our assignments and assessments reflect the learning targets students have had opportunity to learn? If our targets are unclear, or if our assignments and assessments do not reflect them, we are unable to accurately measure levels of student achievement, or to accomplish any of the purposes we may have intended.

Assessment Accuracy *(continued)*

Assessment Design

The third key to accuracy concerns assessment design. Will the assessment give me accurate information about achievement of the learning targets that I can use as I intended to? This key has four parts—four "gatekeepers" to quality. The first gatekeeper is selecting the appropriate assessment method: Do we know how to choose assessment methods to accurately reflect the learning target(s) to be assessed? As educators we often tend to default to our favorite or the most simple to grade assessment method. Or we may defer that decision to the textbook or test publishers, which can limit what kinds of learning we assess. The second gatekeeper is sampling: Do the learning targets represent what was taught? Or what will be taught? Does the relative importance of each learning target match its relative importance during instruction? Is the sample size large enough to inform the decisions intended to be made, or is it part of a larger plan to gather evidence over time? A common error here is to include a mass of targets in a single assessment, producing insufficient data for any one target, which renders the assessment useless for any kind of "data-driven" decision making with regard to content standards mastered or in need of further work. The third gatekeeper is item quality: Do the assessment items themselves, the exercises or tasks, the scoring procedures and scoring guides all adhere to standards of quality? Do we know what to do to fix them when the answer is "No"?

Avoiding Sources of Bias and Distortion

The fourth gatekeeper is avoiding potential sources of bias and distortion: Is there anything in the assessment itself or in the conditions under which it is administered that could lead to inaccurate estimates of student learning? Do we know how to control for these problems in any given assessment method or context? Whether we are selecting or creating an assessment for classroom use, accuracy of results is dependent on the classroom teacher being able to answer each of these gatekeeper questions.

The skill of creating and selecting quality assessments does not come with age or experience. It comes with intentionally working to becoming assessment literate and competent. As we refine our assessment literacy and competency, it is our students who benefit the most.

Source: Adapted with permission from Charles Osborne, Burleson Independent School District, Burleson, TX, 2008.

Personal Reflection:

1. When I use assessments in my classroom, do I consider the accuracy of the instrument? What am I doing to improve its quality?

2. Am I equipped to accurately evaluate the assessments I give?

3. What might I need to learn more about?

READING 3: Developing Assessment Literacy and Competency

Notes for the Discussion Leader:
This reading defines *assessment literacy* as the possession of knowledge about principles of high-quality classroom assessment and *assessment competency* as the ability to apply that knowledge in the classroom to maximize student motivation and achievement. It then explains the learning team approach to developing both assessment literacy and competence, with a rationale for why it is effective.

Developing Assessment Literacy and Competency

Assessment literacy refers to the knowledge and conceptual understanding of the principles of quality classroom assessment. When we possess assessment literacy, we can engage in informed conversation regarding classroom assessment, we can recognize good- and poor-quality assessments and assessment practices, and we can develop quality plans for implementation. *Assessment competency* refers to the consistent practice of high-quality student-involved classroom assessment principles in ways that improve student learning. When we possess assessment competency, we can consistently *apply* the knowledge and understanding of assessment literacy in a variety of classroom settings and thereby have an impact on both student learning and motivation.

For many of us, training in assessment literacy and competency was not part of preservice education. Consequently, we may possess assessment literacy developed on the job, and yet be lacking in assessment competency. As professional educators, each of us bears the responsibility for deepening our own level of expertise. We work in a district that puts great emphasis upon providing professional development, but the responsibility for taking advantage of opportunities to further our capabilities lies with each of us individually.

Hands down, without any reservation, the best method of developing both personal assessment literacy and competency is through active participation in an assessment learning team. This professional development format requires three commitments: (1) to read a portion of the text selected for study; (2) to try one or more ideas out in the classroom; and (3) to meet with colleagues to discuss what you read, what you tried, and what you noticed as a result.

Assessment learning teams focus on the teacher as learner. They meet about every three weeks to review practices in assessment, to discuss reading assignments completed since the last meeting, at times to view videos, to share experiences, and to make plans for the next stages of learning and practice. Learning teams experience the greatest success when all members value and commit both to doing the independent work between meetings and to actively engaging in the collaborative work during meetings. When both of these commitments are in place, assessment learning teams provide the very elements often lacking in other professional development efforts:

- They are ongoing throughout the year, rather than a one-time training.
- They are job embedded and apply to our specific classrooms, grade levels, and subject areas.
- The content and meeting schedule can flex to meet the needs of team members.
- They allow team members to learn from each other as well as from selected resources.

Source: Adapted with permission from Charles Osborne, Burleson Independent School District, Burleson, TX, 2008.

Personal Reflection:

1. What professional development have I participated in that has truly had a positive impact on my classroom practice?

2. What will I do this year to enhance my personal professional development in assessment literacy and competency?

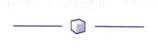

Competency 8

The leader knows and can evaluate teachers' classroom assessment competencies, and helps teachers learn to assess accurately and use the results to benefit student learning.

Evaluating teachers' classroom assessment competence is not yet a norm for many districts. Whether teacher evaluation is summative in nature, using the traditional observational checklists of criteria and indicators, or whether it is a formative model that relies on personal/professional growth goals as the structure for the evaluation, accountability for assessment competence, particularly at the classroom level, is often absent. Whatever supervision and evaluation model is in place, if something is worth knowing and doing properly in the classroom, especially something that can either harm or help students, solid guidance is essential. Specifically, principals need to know how well teachers do the following:

1. Attend to the purpose of each assessment given, who will use the results, and in what way.

2. Address the learning targets being assessed and explain why they are important to assess.

3. Select proper assessment methods for the content.

4. Assure accuracy of the results with good design, proper sampling, and a minimum of bias.

5. Involve students in assessment.

6. Communicate assessment results to meet the needs of a variety of audiences.

7. Provide assessment criteria to students in terms they understand.

8. Provide descriptive feedback to students.

9. Use formative and summative data effectively to guide instruction and improve learning.

When evidence suggests that teachers do these things well a principal knows that high-quality assessment is a priority in the classroom, and that the teacher understands the use of assessment *for* learning to improve student learning. When the principal holds regular discussions with teachers about these practices and is capable of providing supportive, meaningful feedback to staff, regardless of the teacher evaluation model in place, conversations in the school begin to center on the importance of using assessment in ways that contribute to learning, beyond final report card grades.

Principal-teacher discussions can emulate the process we advocate for student-teacher conferences. Principal and teacher exchange views on the teacher's strengths in assessment practices, areas for improvement, and ways to support the teacher in further growth. Sharing descriptive feedback with each other brings teacher and principal together in a professional partnership focused on improved student learning through quality assessment practices. The teacher's professional growth decisions are focused on the goals or targets established during the evaluation meeting.

Expecting students to master standards requires teachers who are competent, confident masters of those standards. Whether hiring new teachers or verifying current teachers' mastery, leaders need to know how to do the verification. If this process identifies teachers who are not masters of the standards they are to teach, leaders must provide a means for these teachers to become competent, confident masters of those standards.

Teaching applicants must answer many questions, both in writing and at interviews. Questions related to classroom management, instructional skill, and issues of student discipline are common. Questions related to the candidate's mastery of content knowledge and development and use of quality assessments necessary for the specific teaching assignment are sometimes overlooked. Frequently, evidence of content mastery and assessment literacy is gathered from college transcripts, previous teaching assignments, or candidate portfolios to help inform the hiring decision.

Success Indicators for Competency 8

The leader

- Explains standards of sound classroom assessment practice that evaluations of teacher performance can/should be based upon.

- Develops interview questions that relate to the classroom assessment literacy of candidates for teaching positions. Knows what questions to ask about assessment quality and the effective use of assessment to promote learning, and is prepared to interpret candidates' answers in terms of their qualifications.

- Creates ways to observe, analyze, evaluate, and provide feedback on classroom assessment process and artifacts (assessment instruments).

Practice with Competency 8

Develop a sample hiring interview and ongoing supervision protocols in the form of questions and "look-for" answers, as well as observational and artifact evaluation plans, and share them with a qualified colleague for review and feedback. (By participating in Activities 22 and 23 you will be well on your way to completing this practice activity.)

Thinking About Assessment

Activity 22: Verifying Teachers' Content Knowledge and Assessment Competence

Purpose:

This activity asks participants to answer three questions: (1) What questions could be asked in an interview with prospective teachers that would help school leaders evaluate their academic preparation to teach and assess the assigned subject(s)? (2) What questions can school leaders ask, or what evidence they should seek, to verify current teachers' mastery of the standards they are expected to teach and their level of assessment literacy in measuring those standards? (3) How would leaders assist teachers who are not currently masters of the standards they are to teach nor competent assessors of these standards to become competent, confident masters and assessors of those standards?

Time:

1 hour

Materials Needed:

- Interview forms and teacher evaluation forms currently in use in your district
- Your district's comprehensive assessment plan, if available
- Interactive whiteboards or flipcharts and easels for capturing discussion points

Suggested Room Setup:

Tables and chairs set up for ease of discussion among participants

Directions:

Think about and discuss the following questions:

- What should you reasonably expect the interview component of the overall hiring process to produce in terms of useful information about the candidate's subject-matter knowledge?

- Given that, what questions could you design that would help inform you about the applicant's subject-matter knowledge? What is the range of acceptable answers to those questions?

- What should you reasonably expect the interview component to produce in terms of useful information about the candidate's assessment competence?

- What questions could you design that would inform you about the applicant's assessment competence? What answers would you consider acceptable for that set of questions?

- Do you currently have a process for determining the subject knowledge and assessment competence of the teachers who already teach in your school or district?

- Is this process adequate?

- Does it need improving? If so, what questions do you need to ask? What evidence do you need to seek?

- What staff development and support do you provide for teachers who are not masters of the standards nor competent assessors of the standards? Is it adequate? What improvements need to be made? Can you assign them to a position where they are masters of the targets their students must master? Can you provide teachers with collaborative learning environments to become assessment literate?

Closure:

Whatever questions you might ask about subject matter knowledge and assessment competence, consider the following points:

- Is there a link between what questions are asked in an employment interview and subsequent teacher evaluation? If not, should there be? Why or why not?

- Is there a link between those same questions, which in part act as expectations of teacher skills and knowledge, and the staff development program of your school or district? If not, should there be? Why or why not?

Look at the questions on some of the interview forms currently in use in your school or district and see if they include questions related to assessment. If they do, are the questions related to assessment *of* learning, assessment *for* learning, or both? If your district has a comprehensive assessment plan, check it to see if it spells out classroom assessment competencies. Also, consider asking teachers whom you believe already understand the principles of quality assessment to tell you what questions they think should be included in the interview.

Thinking About Assessment

Activity 23: Should Teachers Be Held Accountable for Assessment Competence through Evaluation?

Purpose:

Teacher evaluation criteria and instruments vary greatly, and may or may not contain indicators of classroom assessment competence. This leadership team activity asks you as school leaders to think about whether teachers should be evaluated for assessment competence and if so, what the criteria for that evaluation should include. Doing this activity with teacher leaders and union representatives may build ownership and commitment across the administrative and teaching levels of the organization.

Time:

45–60 minutes

Materials Needed:

- Interactive whiteboard or flipchart

- Copies for each participant of the forms you use for teacher evaluation

Suggested Room Setup:

Tables and chairs set for ease of discussion among participants

Directions:

Collect copies of the forms used for teacher evaluation in your school or district. Using the forms, make a separate list of the criteria that relate to assessment competence that are currently included.

In your group, discuss the following question:

Should teachers be held accountable for assessment competence through evaluation?

1. If your answer is "Yes," begin to list criteria, in addition to what may already be included, that you believe should be part of the evaluation document. The criteria would describe the specific knowledge and/or skills that you would want teachers to be able to demonstrate routinely in assessment. In Activity 11, your team members reviewed indicators of sound classroom assessment practice. These same indicators can be underpinnings for the criteria you establish in the evaluation document.

2. If your answer is "No," explain why you do not believe assessment competence should be part of teacher evaluation.

Closure:

This issue, and therefore the activity itself, may be complicated by the fact that many schools and districts no longer use a summative form or process for teacher evaluation. The traditional classroom observation by the principal and checklist with criteria/indicators used for pre-/post-evaluation conferences about individual strengths and areas for improvement has been replaced in some schools. In many cases, new evaluation systems rely more on formative processes, where the teacher selects a few, focused professional-growth goals or instructional goals, sometimes in partnership with the supervisor. Indicators of assessment competence would not necessarily be part of that model or others similar to it. If that is the case in your system, what other ways can schools and districts ensure each teacher is a competent assessor of student learning?

To assist those who wish to add assessment competence to their summative evaluation, the main question to be addressed is, "What are the indicators of competence we want to see demonstrated?" You can compare answers generated in this activity to indicators in several of the other activities in this guide, as well as to the list of principles of assessment *for* learning.

Competency 9

The leader analyzes student assessment information accurately, uses the information to improve curriculum and instruction, and assists teachers in doing the same.

With added levels of testing in the last decade (interim/benchmark, common), students are experiencing more testing than ever. As a result, school leaders have an even greater responsibility for conducting meaningful data analyses and providing clear, accurate reports of student assessment results. State departments of education, local districts, professional organizations, and university preparation programs have helped by providing training for school leaders in test data literacy and use, often offered in the context of the state and/or local testing system. The lessons about assessment quality offered in this guide can be combined with such training to help administrators master this competency.

For those school leaders who have not had access to training programs in the interpretation and use of data to guide improvement, what follows is a high-level overview. For additional and more detailed help, leaders can consult their state department of education and resources such as the following:

The Data Coach's Guide to Improving Learning for All Students: Unleashing the Power of Collaborative Inquiry, Nancy Love, Katherine E. Stiles, Susan Mundry, and Kathryn DiRanna (Thousand Oaks, CA: Corwin, 2008)

Data-driven Decisions and School Leadership: Best Practices for School Improvement, Theodore J. Kowalski, Thomas J. Lasley, and James W. Mahoney (Boston: Pearson/Allyn & Bacon, 2008)

Schools and Data: The Educator's Guide for Using Data to Improve Decision Making, 2nd ed., Theodore B. Creighton (Thousand Oaks, CA: Corwin, 2006)

Show Me the Proof: Tools and Strategies to Make Data Work for You, Stephen White (Englewood, CO: Advanced Learning Press, 2005)

Using Data to Improve Student Learning in School Districts, Victoria L. Bernhardt (Larchmont, NY: Eye on Education, 2006)

In a balanced assessment system, the assessments school leaders are most likely to be involved with are common, interim/benchmark, and annual assessments. Classroom assessments will tend to be interpreted and used by teachers and students.

Common and Interim/Benchmark Assessments

Common, interim/benchmark, and annual assessments are the levels that yield comparable evidence that can therefore be summarized across classrooms or school buildings. If the evidence from these assessments meet certain criteria, they can inform program and faculty improvement decisions that can have a positive impact on student learning. To lead the local development of common or interim/benchmark assessments, school leaders need to be masters of the keys to quality assessment repeatedly referenced in this guide. And, they must be sure their development efforts result in assessments that tell them and their teachers how *each student* did in mastering *each relevant standard*. That means there must be enough instances (test items, tasks, etc.—that is, a big enough sample) in the assessment to lead to a confident conclusion about which students mastered or failed to master each standard. Such results can easily be summarized over students within classrooms or buildings and transformed into information about which standards students consistently struggle to master. These can become the focus of immediate improvement efforts.

After administering a common assessment to students within a grade level or course, teachers can come together to ask many of the same questions asked of the large-scale tests using the data from the common assessments. This assumes that the common assessments were of high quality and the tests were administered and evaluated in a consistent or standardized manner. Common performance assessments, especially, necessitate teachers being trained on the use of the rubric in evaluating student work. Without this, the results would be meaningless because no two teachers would be looking at the same performance in the same way.

Annual Assessments

When analyzing local large-scale annual test results, this same kind of thinking applies as to interim/benchmark assessment results. The driving question should be the same: Which of our state or local standards do our students consistently struggle to master? This is not about averaging annual test scores. It is about looking beneath scores for information that can help schools improve for the sake of the students. The answer to this question will provide a focus for longer-term program and faculty improvement.

The more you can disaggregate or narrow the focus of the scores, the more easily you can pinpoint the strengths and the weaknesses in the performance of groups and individuals, as well as in the standards tested. To analyze data at various levels of assessment and to communicate the information to all who need it, many principals form school data teams. These teams, comprised of representatives of the building's instructional staff (and sometimes parents as well), are given the responsibility for collecting the data and examining the results to help determine what can be learned about student performance. If your annual or interim/benchmark assessment gives you evidence of student mastery of each standard (which we believe it should) then interpretation at this level asks the following:

- On which standards do our students perform well?

- On which standards do our students perform poorly?

- Have there been significant changes from year to year?

- What generalizations can we make from this data about student performance?

Following are additional questions to consider:

- What content areas show evidence of higher or lower achievement than others?

- Looking at previous years' scores, what trends are indicated in the content area scores? (up, down, little change?)

- Did we test all eligible students? Did we increase or decrease the percentage of students tested?

- In what areas are students farthest from being proficient? In what areas are students closest to being proficient?

- What activities or strategies appear to have contributed to these findings? What strategies or activities seem to have had no effect?

- What, if any gap exists in student performance among groups by gender, ethnicity, economic status, English as a second language, or special education? Are the gaps greater or lesser in any content area?

- How do students perform who are new to our schools/district? How do our students perform who have been in our schools/district for an extended time?

- Are the test results consistent with other tests given in school? Are they consistent with report card grades/GPAs?

- Has our school or district implemented any professional development activities that have had measurable impact on these results?

- In what areas is student performance improving? Not improving?

- Is there a particular assessment method that appears to cause students difficulty?

- What do the data from our feeder school(s) suggest?

- Are the test results from one test consistent with other tests given in the school? Are they consistent with report card grades/GPAs?

- What needs for improvement can we infer from the data?

- What is currently in place that addresses those needs?

- How do the results for our school compare with other groups—schools, district, state?

- What else do we need to know, and what data do we need to get the answers?

Success Indicators for Competency 9

The leader

- Understands the meaning of the results of all tests used in the school and how to interpret them correctly.

- Knows how to turn assessment results into useful information and how to link them directly to instructional decision making at classroom, interim/benchmark, and annual levels of assessment use.

Practice with Competency 9

Leaders can help put any standardized test in context by identifying the match between standardized test content and what students are learning through the local curriculum, identifying what specific standards each score represents, and helping teachers use the test information appropriately. Select one of the standardized tests used in your building/district, and by using the table of test specifications available from the publisher, create an alignment table between what is assessed on the test and your district or state written curriculum.

Return to your assessment audit from Activity 4 in Part 3 of this guide. The completed audit provides information about each test currently used, including the purposes for giving the test, the standards assessed, and how the results will be used. Using that list of assessments, see which ones provide scores you can interpret and use for instructional improvement, and which ones would require more familiarity on your part in order to use for that purpose. Select one of these and develop a plan for how to become more literate about that test's scores and possible uses.

Competency 10

The leader develops and implements sound assessment and assessment-related policies.

Policy drives practice. If leaders want quality assessment practices in every classroom then district and school policies must support the implementation and continued use of such practices.

Many policies at both the school and the district level have the potential to either support or hinder the effective use of sound assessment practice. Further, policies can either support each other, acting in concert as a system of beliefs and practices, or they can act in opposition to each other, creating inconsistency and even conflict. It is part of the school leader's assessment responsibilities to revise policies so they provide a framework for sound practice and act in unison with each other. In fact, without policy support, assessment reform initiatives may flounder. Leaders are more likely to succeed at this task if they approach it with three perspectives in mind:

> *Policy drives practice. If leaders want quality assessment practices in every classroom then district and school policies must support the implementation and continued use of such practices.*

1. How leaders view the role of the policy manual is critical. School and district policy needs to be seen as more than the regulatory compliance arm of the organization. Beyond fulfilling the legal requirements of the state and federal governments, policy can serve as an implementation tool for strategic planning efforts and can be used as one of many strategies to help the vision become reality. It provides an opportunity to set and communicate standards, expectations, and the priorities most relevant to student achievement, and can help educate the local community. The integration of district planning and priorities with policy making is especially necessary in a standards-based assessment system (California School Boards Association, 1999).

2. Assessment systems need to be planned as just that: systems with connected parts all working toward a common goal. District policy manuals and faculty handbooks should be approached from the same perspective. The elements all need to fit together, which requires thinking about policies beyond revising one at a time or revising each only in response to some district crisis or legislative enactment.

3. A written comprehensive assessment plan, based in part on the Seven Actions presented in this guide, clarifies the purpose of assessment and how it fits into effective teaching and learning. Essential for assessment reform is a document that states assessment beliefs and provides guiding principles and policies for both large-scale testing and classroom practice based on that set of beliefs.

Policies that have a strong connection with student assessment and that should be reviewed for appropriateness and congruence include the following:

- Curriculum development
- Curriculum adoption
- Assessment
- Grading
- Professional development
- Hiring
- Teacher evaluation
- Student placement
- Communicating student progress
- Program evaluation
- IEP
- Strategic planning
- Pupil records
- Attendance
- Grouping for instruction
- Gifted/talented
- Lesson planning
- Promotion and retention
- Parent involvement
- Student selection
- Remediation and intervention
- Accountability
- Instruction
- Graduation requirements
- Homework
- Instructional materials

Success Indicators for Competency 10

The leader

- Knows the policies that contribute to assessment balance, quality and effective use, and is able to draft those statements for review, evaluation, and adoption.

- Knows how to translate policies into procedures and guidelines that honor the intent of the policy.

Practice with Competency 10

Draft a sample assessment philosophy that reflects your vision. Then make a list of the various places in the district and building policy manual where policies might need reevaluation or where key policies might be missing and need to be written. For each location, try drafting the needed policy statement.

Thinking About Assessment

Activity 24: Using School/District Policies to Support Quality Assessment

Purpose:

This activity requests that your team review a series of school/district policies, all of which have a connection in some way to assessment. Some are more complete than others; some are more current and better written than others. All are examples of policies at the district level, although school-level administrators can also make use of this activity simply by shifting the emphasis to school-level policies contained in a faculty handbook. By reviewing the policies with an eye toward how they could be rewritten or improved to be more supportive of quality assessment, your team practices building the framework to help support quality assessment.

One of the objectives of this activity and in working with policy in general is to see policies as a systemic whole, where the elements (in this case the policies themselves) hang together, all working toward a common purpose. Not approaching the policy manual in that way risks having policies in opposition to each other: an attendance policy may contradict a grading policy, or a promotion/retention policy may conflict with a policy on student assessment that is grounded in a specific set of belief statements.

Lastly, the district-level policies in this activity are just that; some context is missing without the implementation procedures that usually accompany policies and provide the specifics of how the policy is to be applied. However, the underlying concepts and ideas are apparent in each example. The intention of the activity is not to perfect each policy, but rather to get some practice in reviewing policies with quality assessment as the filter.

Time:

90 minutes

Materials Needed:

Optional: policies from your school or district

Suggested Room Setup:

Tables and chairs

Directions:

Before starting this activity, it will be helpful for your team to list a set of criteria to use when reviewing these policies (and any other policies you may choose to use from your local school or district). What is the group looking to achieve in assessment through school or district policies? What would constitute a strong policy? For example, your team might generate policy review criteria in the form of questions. The list that follows is a start, but other considerations may be important to your team.

Does this policy

- Support the vision of assessment in the school or district?

- Have a direct impact on student learning?

- Have an impact on or connection to other policies that need to be considered?

- Encourage the use of multiple measures of student learning, creating judgments made about students with combinations of data sources?

- Require clear, meaningful, and frequent communication about learning?

- Link standards, instruction, and assessment?

- Require any specialized professional development?

Recognize that each of these criteria or those your team may generate might not be relevant or apply to each policy under review. After finalizing your list of criteria, read the first policy in this activity. Then pause and consider the following three questions with your team. Do this with the remainder of the sample policies in this activity. Use the criteria developed by your team to help answer the questions for each policy review.

1. What are the strong points of the policy the way it is currently written?

2. What are the weak areas of the policy?

3. What language could be omitted, and what language might be added to make it more supportive of sound assessment?

Policy 2101—Student Retention/Promotion

As the ability to read proficiently is the basic foundation for success in school, as it is indeed throughout life, it is the goal of the primary school, the first three (3) grades, to teach each child to read independently with understanding by the time he/she finishes the third grade. It is within this period when retention of a youngster in a grade can be most valuable. Teachers, taking into account factors such as achievement, mental age, chronological age, emotional stability, social and physical maturity may find it advisable in the case of some students to retain a child once or twice during this period. By following this policy, the District will find some children completing the first three grades in four (4) years and some in five (5) as well as the majority who will finish in the regular three (3) year period.

With the above as a basic policy, retention after the third grade should only be a problem in those cases where a student is not achieving and meeting the grade standards of which he is capable. In cases where it is contemplated holding a student in the same grade for an extra year, the teacher should notify the parents as early in the year as possible, but not later than the end of the third quarter.

No student shall be retained for more than two (2) years in the same grade.

Since it is the responsibility of the school to adjust the work in each grade to the child's individual needs and ability to provide an equal educational opportunity for all children, no arbitrary policy of promotion is suggested. Promotion should be made for grade to grade, based upon a consideration of the best interest of the student concerned.

The following factors shall be taken into consideration: achievement, mental age, chronological age, emotional stability, social and physical maturity. The curriculum should be so broad on each grade level that the needs of bright students are met, as well as the needs of average and slow students. Therefore, when accepting pupils who are new to District schools, the principal should make the best placement possible on the basis of the information he/she can obtain.

Policy 2102—Lesson Plans

To ensure proper planning and continuity of instruction, the Board requires that each teacher prepare lesson plans for daily instruction. To facilitate more effective instruction, lesson plans must be prepared in advance of the actual class presentation. The format for the lesson plan will be specified by the building principal and shall be reviewed on a regular basis. The plan book must be readily available when a substitute teacher is needed.

Policy 2103—Class Rank

The Board acknowledges the usefulness of a system of computing grade point averages and class ranking for secondary school graduates to inform students, parents, and others of their relative academic placement among their peers.

The Board authorizes a system of class ranking, by grade point average, for student in grades 9–12. Class rank shall be computed by the final grade except that non-numerical marks/grades shall be excluded from the calculation of the grade point average.

A student's grade point average shall be reported on his/her term grade report. Such calculations may also be used for recognizing individual students for their achievement.

Policy 2104—Homework

The Board believes that homework is a constructive tool in the teaching/learning process when geared to the age, health, abilities, and needs of students. Purposeful assignments not only enhance student achievement but also develop self-discipline and associated good working habits. As an extension of the classroom, homework must be planned and organized; must be viewed as purposeful to the students; and must be evaluated and returned to the student in a timely manner.

The purposes of homework assignments, the basis for evaluating the work performed and the guidelines and/or rules should be made clear to the student at the time of the assignment.

The school principal shall establish guidelines that clarify the nature and use of homework assignments to improve school achievement.

Make-up work, due to illness, is not to be considered as homework. Students shall be given the opportunity to make up assignments missed during excused absences.

Policy 2106—Grading and Progress Reports

The Board believes that the cooperation of school and home is a vital ingredient in the growth and education of the student and recognizes the responsibility to keep parents informed of student personal development/work habits, as well as academic progress in school.

The issuance of grades and progress reports on a regular basis serves as the basis for continuous evaluation of the student's performance and determining changes that should be made to effect improvement. These reports shall be designed to provide information that will be helpful to the student, teacher, counselor, and parent. For grades 9–12, the district shall comply with the marking/grading system incorporated into the statewide standardized high school transcript. The superintendent may consider alternative grading/progress reports. A student's grade point shall be reported for each term, individually and cumulatively.

The Board directs the superintendent to establish a system of reporting student progress and shall require all staff members to comply with such a system as a part of their teaching responsibility.

If classroom participation is used as the basis of mastery of an objective, a student's grades may be adversely affected by an absence, provided that on the day of the excused absence, there was a graded participation activity. If the teacher does not so advise students in writing, the teacher may not use attendance and participation in the grading process. Teachers shall consider circumstances pertaining to the student's inability to attend school. No student grade shall be reduced or credit denied for disciplinary reasons only, rather than for academic reasons, unless due process of law is provided. Individual students, who feel that an unjust application of attendance or tardiness factors has been made, may follow the appeal process for resolving the differences. Academic appeals have no further step for appeal.

Policy 2107—Instruction

Effective Communication about Student Achievement

_____ School District is a standards driven district with the goal of communicating effectively about student achievement. It is the intent of the District to provide timely, understandable, and meaningful information about student progress towards clearly articulated achievement standards to students, parents, educational professionals, and third parties with interest. Grading and reporting practices represent one of a variety of ways to communicate student progress towards standards and may serve the following purpose(s).

* Communication of the achievement status of students to parents/guardians in ways that describe progress toward district standards and provide an accurate focus on learning.

* Information students can use for self-evaluation and improvement.

* Data for the selection, identification, or grouping of students for certain educational paths or programs.

* Information for evaluation of the effectiveness of instructional programs.

Grading and reporting provide important information about student progress, but there is no single best way of communicating about student achievement. The District will use a variety of ways to deliver information about student achievement to intended users. All information users are important and are entitled to timely and accurate achievement data: some may require greater detail about achievement than can be provided by grades and test scores to make informed decisions. The following illustrate different types of communication about student achievement:

- Checklists of standards
- Narrative descriptions
- Portfolios of various kinds
- Report card grades
- Student conferences

All practices related to communication about student achievement should be carried out according to the best current understanding and application of the research. The District will provide staff members on-going professional development needed to gain that understanding.

Grading and Reporting

The District's policy and procedures on communication about student achievement, specifically grading and reporting practices, are based upon the principles that

- Individual achievement of clearly stated learning targets should be the only basis for grades, providing an accurate reflection of what each student knows and can do; the effectiveness of the communication is determined by the accuracy of the information about student achievement.

- Other characteristics (effort, behavior, attendance, attitude, etc.) should not be included in grades but should be reported separately.

- Different users and decision makers of achievement data need information in different forms at different times in order to make their decisions.

- Grading and reporting should always be done in reference to specified achievement targets, comparing students' performance against a standard rather than against other students in the class (on a curve).

- Grades should be calculated to ensure that the grade each student receives is a fair reflection of what he/she knows and can do, emphasizing the most recent summative assessment information.

- Consideration shall be given to the use of appropriate grade calculation procedures to ensure that assigned grades reflect the intended importance of each leaning goal.

- Grades have some value as incentives but no value as punishments.

During the first week of classes, teachers shall provide students and parents with a written syllabus of learning expectations and grading criteria in clear, easily understandable language, indicating how summative assessment throughout the grading period will be calculated into course grades. Teachers shall discuss classroom assessment practices with students, in an age appropriate manner, at the beginning of instruction.

The Superintendent shall develop written procedures that support the District policy on Communicating Effectively about Student Achievement.

Thinking About Assessment
Activity 25: A Self-analysis for School Leaders

Purpose:

Up to this point you have largely worked with your leadership study team members. This activity asks you to reflect individually on the ten competencies using the following two questions:

1. Each of the Ten Assessment Competencies for School Leaders offers many ways for principals to demonstrate proficiency. With the list of Competencies in front of you (p. 198), examine each one in relation to your knowledge and actions as a school leader. Try to attach specific examples to each Competency that you carry out as the assessment leader in the school.

2. Using the worksheet, "Assessment Competencies for School Leaders" (p. 198), rate yourself on the Ten Competencies. What areas stand out as your strengths? Which one(s) could you target for improvement?

Assessment Competencies for School Leaders

1. The leader understands the attributes of a sound and balanced assessment system, and the conditions required to achieve balance in local systems.

    Low   1 _____   2 _____   3 _____   4 _____   5 _____   *High*

2. The leader understands the necessity of clear academic achievement standards, aligned classroom-level achievement targets, and their relationship to the development of accurate assessments.

    Low   1 _____   2 _____   3 _____   4 _____   5 _____   *High*

3. The leader understands the standards of quality for student assessments, helps teachers learn to assess accurately and use the results productively, and ensures that these standards are met in all school/district assessments.

    Low   1 _____   2 _____   3 _____   4 _____   5 _____   *High*

4. The leader knows assessment *for* learning practices and works with staff to integrate them into classroom instruction.

    Low   1 _____   2 _____   3 _____   4 _____   5 _____   *High*

5. The leader creates the conditions necessary for the appropriate use and reporting of student achievement information, and can communicate effectively with all members of the school community about student assessment results, including report card grades, and their relationship to improving curriculum and instruction.

    Low   1 _____   2 _____   3 _____   4 _____   5 _____   *High*

6. The leader understands the issues related to the unethical and inappropriate use of student assessment and protects students and staff from such misuse.

    Low   1 _____   2 _____   3 _____   4 _____   5 _____   *High*

7. The leader can plan, present and/or secure professional development activities that contribute to the use of sound assessment practices.

    Low   1 _____   2 _____   3 _____   4 _____   5 _____   *High*

8. The leader knows and can evaluate the teacher's classroom assessment competencies, and helps teachers learn to assess accurately and use the results productively.

    Low   1 _____   2 _____   3 _____   4 _____   5 _____   *High*

9. The leader analyzes student assessment information accurately, uses the information to improve curriculum and instruction, and assists teachers in doing the same.

    Low   1 _____   2 _____   3 _____   4 _____   5 _____   *High*

10. The leader develops and implements sound assessment and assessment-related policies.

    Low   1 _____   2 _____   3 _____   4 _____   5 _____   *High*

Planning for Action

STUDENT
SUCCESS

Teacher
Competencies

Planning
for
Action

Required Skills
for Assessment
Balance and Quality

The Path to Assessment
Balance and Quality

Building the Vision

Laying the Foundation

The Building Blocks of Assessment Success

Planning for Action

5

An assessment system that is in balance will ensure that the right kind of information is used for the right purpose, always in the service of improved student learning. Through the use of high-quality assessments *of* and *for* learning linked to the targets of instruction, students will be able to show both what they know and can do, and play a key role in managing their own success. The final part of this guide helps you synthesize the thinking and work of your leadership study team from Parts 1 through 4 into a plan of action that moves the vision of your assessment system closer to reality. At this point, you have developed some ideas about the current status of your system. You also may have formed opinions about the level of your own assessment literacy and about the professional development needs of your instructional staff. Before acting on those conclusions, there are three final activities to complete, each of which will help you think about connections between this scope of work and other school/district initiatives and frameworks for school leadership.

Thinking About Assessment

Activity 26: Making Connections between Leadership Competencies and the Seven Actions

Purpose:

We believe that the successful completion of the Seven Actions of Part 3 is in part dependent on mastery of the Ten Assessment Competencies for School Leaders of Part 4. The purpose of this activity is to make these connections explicit, encouraging you to move forward with them to develop your own assessment competence as needed.

Time:

One hour

Materials Needed:

A copy of Table 5-1 and access to the list of Ten Assessment Competencies for School Leaders (found on the accompanying CD-ROM)

Suggested Room Setup:

Tables and chairs

Directions:

Working as a team, review each Action one at a time by studying its row in the table, working from left to right. When you reach the right column, study the list of competencies and discuss which of them relate to the successful completion of that Action. When you have completed your discussion of all Seven Actions, compare your results to the key at the bottom of the table. This key identifies minimum possible connections—you may see other connections.

Table 5-1 **The Leadership Competencies Underpinning the Seven Assessment Actions**

Action Steps in Assessment to Ensure Student Success	Enduring Belief(s) to Abandon	New Practice to Be Implemented	Locus of Control for Needed Action	Which Leader Competencies Relate?*
1. Balance Assessment Systems	Annual standardized and interim/benchmark tests offer best support for school improvement.	Classroom assessments have been proven by research to be valuable in improving student learning; so balance the three.	School district leaders are responsible for balance in their local assessment systems.	
2. Refine Achievement Standards	State standards represent a sufficient definition of student learning.	Standards need to be manageable in number; add clarity where needed; articulate over grade levels; deconstruct each into everyday learning targets; transform those into student-friendly language.	States and local school district leaders must refine learner expectations.	
3. Ensure Assessment Quality	Classroom and other assessments are already of high quality, or it doesn't matter.	We must ensure the quality of all assessments by verifying it locally.	University preservice training and district professional development programs focused on quality assessment practices are essential.	
4. Use Assessment *for* Learning Strategies	Assessment is only something that teachers and school leaders do.	Recognize that students assess their own achievement too, and make decisions based on their interpretations of results.	Only teachers can make students productive assessment users within their classrooms.	
5. Build Communication Systems	Evaluative feedback such as report card grades and test scores represent effective communication capable of encouraging student learning.	Descriptive feedback is needed when its purpose is to support learning; evaluative feedback must be based on sound practice.	Only teachers can balance the use of descriptive and evaluative feedback in their classrooms.	

Table 5-1 **The Leadership Competencies Underpinning the Seven Assessment Actions** *(continued)*

Action Steps in Assessment to Ensure Student Success	Enduring Belief(s) to Abandon	New Practice to Be Implemented	Locus of Control for Needed Action	Which Leader Competencies Relate?*
6. Motivate Students with Learning Success	The intimidation of accountability motivates all learners.	Success at learning is the motivator that can work for all students.	Only teachers can use the classroom assessment process to keep students believing in themselves as learners.	
7. Promote Assessment Literacy	Teachers and principals already are assessment literate, or it doesn't matter if they are.	Teachers and school leaders need the assessment knowledge and skill shown to improve student learning.	Only policy makers and district leaders can set priorities and allocate resources to provide teachers and school leaders the opportunity to become assessment literate.	

Answer Key:	Action	Competencies	Action	Competencies
	1	1	5	1–5
	2	2	6	1–6
	3	1–3	7	1–10
	4	1–4		

Thinking About Assessment

Activity 27: Making Connections between a District's Current Direction and Assessment Literacy

Purpose:

Planning for assessment balance and quality, including professional development in assessment literacy, can be seen as "just one more thing we should do." This activity will help you see how assessment is related to and can support other district initiatives as opposed to being an isolated "add-on." The goal is to state the connection between your local direction/initiative and assessment literacy clearly, so others may also understand the role assessment literacy plays in program and student success.

Time:

30–60 minutes, depending on the number of initiatives and documents you choose to analyze

Materials Needed:

- Copies of or digital access to any of the following:
    — District's vision or mission statement

    — Belief statements

    — Graduation expectations for students

    — Strategic planning priorities and goals

- List of the common initiatives within your district, such as
    — Developing local standards-based assessment systems, aligned with state standards

    — Aligning instruction with standards

    — Differentiation of instruction

    — Response to intervention

    — Curriculum mapping

    — Professional Learning Communities

    — Formative assessment

    — Closing the achievement gap

    — Improving instruction in the content areas

    — Improving teacher quality

    — Developing standards-based report cards

Suggested Room Setup:

A circle or U-shaped seating arrangement where individual reflections and large-group discussion can take place

Directions:

- First, as a team, agree to focus on one of your initiatives or directional documents, probably one is that is driving most of the work by the district's members or is perceived as the most important.

- As individuals, engage in a personal reflection based on the following question (5–10 minutes):

    What role would/could a foundation of assessment literacy and the effective use of quality classroom assessment play in the success of this initiative or in meeting our district or school goals? That is, what points could I make to explain how assessment underpins the effectiveness of the initiative or the accomplishment of the mission/vision?

- Group discussion (10–15 minutes): Discuss individual reflections. Note similarities and differences among the team members' thoughts.

- As a team, summarize your discussion (10–15 minutes). Draw conclusions and develop talking points on how the pursuit of quality, balanced practices can bring the district closer to improving student learning for all.

- Work with other directional documents or school initiatives and repeat the individual and group processing steps. Note commonalities among the initiatives. This will make it clear that many school initiatives or directions can reach their potential only when accompanied by sound classroom assessment.

Thinking About Assessment

Activity 28: Linking the Ten Assessment Competencies for School Leaders with the 2008 ISLLC Educational Leadership Policy Standards and the Twenty-one Principal Leadership Responsibilities

Purpose:

2008 ISLLC Educational Leadership Policy Standards: The majority of states use the Interstate School Leaders Licensure Consortium (ISLLC) as their framework for the preparation of educational leaders. Although assessment is not dealt with in great detail in the standards (Council of Chief State School Officers, 2008), accurate assessment is required to achieve many of the standards, and assessment *for* learning classroom practices might also prove beneficial to accomplishment of some.

Twenty-one Principal Leadership Responsibilities: Waters, Marzano, and McNulty (2003) and Waters and Cameron (2007) identify twenty-one responsibilities of school leaders. In their meta-analyses they looked for specific behaviors related to principal leadership and their positive impact on student learning. We see a synergy between the Twenty-one Principal Leadership Responsibilities and the Ten Assessment Competencies for School Leaders. Competencies 1, 2, 3, and 4 center on the school leader understanding the attributes of a quality, balanced assessment program, having the ability to communicate that vision to teachers and other members of the school community, and ensuring that quality assessment principles are practiced in all classrooms. This calls for school leaders who are change agents, have well-defined beliefs around quality assessment practices, and know what quality assessment practices look like. They can communicate those beliefs effectively and are involved in helping teachers and others acquire assessment literacy throughout the organization.

The 2008 ISLLC Educational Leadership Policy Standards, the set of Twenty-one Principal Leadership Responsibilities, and the Ten Assessment Competencies are related in focusing school leaders on improved student achievement through a defined set of behaviors. Engaging in these behaviors will assist school leaders in implementing the Seven Actions presented in this guide.

Time:

About an hour

Materials Needed:

- Interactive whiteboard, flipchart

- Printed copies of the 2008 ISLLC Standards, Twenty-one Principal Leadership Responsibilities, and the Ten Assessment Competencies for School Leaders (found on the accompanying CD-ROM)

- Copies of the accompanying graphic organizer for all participants (a version suitable for writing in appears on the CD-ROM)

Suggested Room Setup:

Tables and chairs set for easy discussion among small groups of school leaders

Directions:

If you are doing this activity alone or your leadership team is small, choose either the 2008 ISLLC Educational Leadership Policy Standards or the Twenty-one Principal Leadership Responsibilities and find the connections to the Ten Assessment Competencies for School Leaders. If your leadership team is larger, then ask one-half of the team to focus on the ISLLC Standards and the other half on the Leadership Responsibilities. Later each group can share their findings with the other and make further connections among the three sets of behaviors. Print out the following graphic organizer to note and help keep track of those connections.

Finding the connections:

1. Which assessment competencies will promote meeting the 2008 ISLLC Educational Leadership Policy Standards?

2. By meeting the ISLLC standards, which assessment competencies are further developed?

3. Which Principal Leadership Responsibilities will promote the acquisition of the Ten Assessment Competencies?

4. By acquiring the Ten Assessment Competencies, which Principal Leadership Responsibilities are further developed?

2008 ISLLC Educational Leadership Policy Standards	ATI Assessment Competencies for School Leaders 2009	Twenty-one Principal Leadership Responsibilities

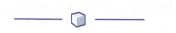

Action Planning for Assessment Balance and Quality

Where Are We Trying to Go with Our Assessment System?

Through the activities in this guide you have been reflecting on and discussing your current situation as well as your vision for the future, thinking about where you want your district or school to be relative to student assessment. If the future still seems unclear to you, revisit Activity 1 in Part 2.

Where Are We Now?

The second question—where you are now—was addressed in Part 3's discussion of the Seven Actions. When you completed the District Assessment System Self-Evaluation at the end of Part 3, you drew a picture of the current status of your assessment system. You identified what work has already been done and in what areas, what work is underway, and what work remains. Other indicators of work yet to be done may become evident through team discussions or from other sections of this Action Guide. The analysis of your own professional knowledge and skills relative to the Ten Assessment Competencies for School Leaders in Part 4 may also influence how you prioritize what comes next. Your team's profile may point to the need for a clearer, well-written curriculum, or to the need to communicate more accurately and efficiently about student achievement. Each leadership team will be in a different place, with perhaps multiple priorities.

How Can We Close the Gap between the Two?

What is needed now are specific answers to the third and final question: "How can we close the gap?" To answer, you must transfer to a written action plan your team's analysis of your current system and priorities for a new system. The work will vary based on the profile you created. Some leadership teams will be able to take action on their own; others may want to bring into the process a larger group of district or school stakeholders. Still others may first need to educate their peers or the instructional staff about the need for and promise of assessment balance and quality.

Like the district curriculum guide that can collect dust on top of the file cabinet, there is no guarantee that action plans will fulfill their promise. But just as you can raise the probability that the written district curriculum is also the taught, tested, and learned curriculum, you also can increase the likelihood that your action plans for assessment will succeed. Here's how:

- Ensure your plan is grounded in the clear vision your team refined over the course of its study, using well-articulated beliefs about assessment as the foundation for that vision.

- Use the Seven Actions self-analysis to focus on results by identifying long-term goals and specific, achievable milestones to chart the progress of your plan.

  - Develop clear strategies aimed at reaching the goals and milestones with the required funding and other resources identified and allocated, if applicable.

  - Identify the staff development required for teachers and administrators and plan for it to be readily available.

  - Recognize and communicate to others that the plan's sole purpose is to improve student learning, making it even more difficult to leave on a shelf.

Ensure your plan is grounded in the clear vision your team refined over the course of its study, using well-articulated beliefs about assessment as the foundation for that vision.

If your school or district has a preferred planning process used successfully in the past, or has a series of planning templates for documenting the goals and objectives, or follows a policy that guides the makeup of a planning team, we encourage your leadership team to put those tools to use here. Success of the plan is paramount; flexibility in its content, creation, and documentation is important to that success. If you have no preferred process, let us propose one for you.

Prioritizing the Actions to Take

As you begin planning you may ask, Where do we start? What should we do first, second, third . . . ? The following questions may help as you consider the options:

- What will be quickest or easiest to do immediately?

  The focus here is finding a scope of work that can be accomplished quickly yet contribute to realizing the vision. For example, if your district has identified student achievement standards, but they are written in language that may be difficult for students or their families to understand, you can rewrite them into student- or family-friendly language, post them online or print them in the parent handbook, and regularly share them with students. This will immediately help both students and their parents. Students know where they are headed in their learning, and their parents will be better able to follow their children's progress and provide better ongoing feedback.

- What will have the most impact?

  Examine your action plan and discuss the potential effect of your proposed actions. For example, you may decide that because quality professional development around assessment literacy is the underpinning of all Seven Actions, refining your professional development program will have the greatest impact.

- What actions are prerequisites to others?

  Ensuring all staff understand the difference between assessment *of* and *for* learning may be the starting place for your system because identifying the purpose for assessing is prerequisite to ensuring assessment quality.

- What actions will support other district goals to improve learning?

  Assessment literacy can bring coherence and support to your district's or school's established learning goals. Say, for example, that based on current state test information on reading you realize you need to address your district reading program. Establishing reading learning targets and assessing them to understand what each of your students already know and need to learn are the first steps to identifying and implementing needed interventions.

Discussion centered on these and similar questions can assist you in determining what actions to take first.

Action Planning Templates

To help you complete your action plan we have included sample planning templates for each of the Seven Actions.

Top Section of the Action Planning Template

The top section of each of the seven templates that follow (pp. 212–215; copies suitable for writing in appear on the accompanying CD-ROM) crosses the various roles and levels in the organization of a school system. It is designed to help your team think about all of the different levels and positions in the organization that could be called on to contribute to the plan's success. The intent is to foster thinking that reaches from the classroom to the boardroom in the design of your action plan. As an example: think about Action 1, and the work you need to do to balance your district assessment system. Within each cell of the table, enter what responsibilities fall to each player at each level. What is the school board's job relative to assessment balance, if any? The superintendent's? The teachers'?

Bottom Section of the Action Planning Template

The bottom section of each template is the action planning tool where you specify exactly what is to be done to create assessment balance and quality. Your team may have one goal for each of the Seven Actions, or several goals for each, depending entirely on your District Assessment System Self-Evaluation results. List here those activities supporting each goal for each of the Seven Actions, describing the intended outcome, specific tasks required, the person(s) responsible, required resources, and the timeline for accomplishment. Copy as many pages as needed per Action to accommodate the scope of work.

Assessment *of* and *for* Learning

Action 1: Balance Your Assessment System

Roles and Responsibilities			
Position	District Level	School Level	Classroom Level
School Board			
Superintendent			
Curriculum Director			
Principals			
C & I/Prof. Dev. Support Staff			
Teachers			

Action Plan Goal						
Proposed Action(s)	Intended Outcome	Specific Task(s)	Evidence of Accomplishment	Person(s) Resp.	Resources Required	Due Date

Assessment *of* and *for* Learning

Action 2: Refine Achievement Standards

Roles and Responsibilities			
Position	District Level	School Level	Classroom Level
School Board			
Superintendent			
Curriculum Director			
Principals			
C & I/Prof. Dev. Support Staff			
Teachers			

Action Plan Goal						
Proposed Action(s)	Intended Outcome	Specific Task(s)	Evidence of Accomplishment	Person(s) Resp.	Resources Required	Due Date

Assessment *of* and *for* Learning

Action 3: Ensure Assessment Quality

Roles and Responsibilities			
Position	District Level	School Level	Classroom Level
School Board			
Superintendent			
Curriculum Director			
Principals			
C & I/Prof. Dev. Support Staff			
Teachers			

Action Plan Goal						
Proposed Action(s)	Intended Outcome	Specific Task(s)	Evidence of Accomplishment	Person(s) Resp.	Resources Required	Due Date

Assessment *of* and *for* Learning

Action 4: Help Learners Become Assessors by Using Assessment for *Learning Strategies in the Classroom*

Roles and Responsibilities			
Position	District Level	School Level	Classroom Level
School Board			
Superintendent			
Curriculum Director			
Principals			
C & I/Prof. Dev. Support Staff			
Teachers			

Action Plan Goal						
Proposed Action(s)	Intended Outcome	Specific Task(s)	Evidence of Accomplishment	Person(s) Resp.	Resources Required	Due Date

Assessment *of* and *for* Learning

Action 5: Build Communication Systems That Both Support and Report Learning

Roles and Responsibilities			
Position	District Level	School Level	Classroom Level
School Board			
Superintendent			
Curriculum Director			
Principals			
C & I/Prof. Dev. Support Staff			
Teachers			

Action Plan Goal						
Proposed Action(s)	Intended Outcome	Specific Task(s)	Evidence of Accomplishment	Person(s) Resp.	Resources Required	Due Date

Assessment *of* and *for* Learning

Action 6: Motivate Students with Learning Success

Roles and Responsibilities			
Position	District Level	School Level	Classroom Level
School Board			
Superintendent			
Curriculum Director			
Principals			
C & I/Prof. Dev. Support Staff			
Teachers			

Action Plan Goal						
Proposed Action(s)	Intended Outcome	Specific Task(s)	Evidence of Accomplishment	Person(s) Resp.	Resources Required	Due Date

Assessment *of* and *for* Learning

Action 7: Promote the Development of Assessment Literacy

Roles and Responsibilities			
Position	District Level	School Level	Classroom Level
School Board			
Superintendent			
Curriculum Director			
Principals			
C & I/Prof. Dev. Support Staff			
Teachers			

Action Plan Goal						
Proposed Action(s)	Intended Outcome	Specific Task(s)	Evidence of Accomplishment	Person(s) Resp.	Resources Required	Due Date

Additional Planning Considerations

Following are other issues your team may want to consider either while developing your action plan or in future review and planning.

The Comprehensive Assessment Plan

The action planning process and templates in this guide will help your team focus on improving assessment balance and quality while emphasizing the role assessment *for* learning can and should play in the total system. Although similar in some respects, it is not the same as developing a school/district comprehensive assessment plan, which you may already have. A comprehensive assessment plan helps manage the assessment business of the school or district and acts as a guide for all issues related to testing, assessment, and monitoring the progress of all students. Issues such as appropriate student placement in special programs, testing accommodations for special populations, total system costs, test materials maintenance and security, technical and legal issues, student promotion and retention, and the information needs, sources, and models for program evaluation are examples of topics addressed in a comprehensive assessment plan. Those types of issues may or may not find their way into your assessment *for* learning action plan; if they do not, remember that they can and should be addressed and communicated to staff in some way.

A comprehensive assessment plan helps manage the assessment business of the school or district and acts as a guide for all issues related to testing, assessment, and monitoring the progress of all students.

Helping Policy Makers Understand Balance and Quality

We've worked in this guide at the school and district policy levels, trying to make sure policies drive sound practice and support quality assessment at those levels. But there are other levels of policy you might also want to consider trying to influence in the same way. Policy makers, not just at the local school board level but also at the state and federal level, need a deep understanding of assessment issues if they are to assist schools and districts achieve balance and quality. Knowing the limitations of standardized testing, and also knowing the quality information and data that assessment-literate teachers can produce about individual students is an important start for policy makers at these levels. Further, they need to understand the role of professional development in improving schools and in achieving standards-based systems. Without that, educators will continue to be left without opportunity to learn and apply assessment *for* learning strategies in the classroom.

Communicating and Monitoring the Plan

The success of many reform efforts is due as much to the collaboration used to develop the strategic plan and to effectively communicating the plan to all stakeholders as it is to the plan's actual goals and content. Your leadership team should consider strategies for generating support for improvement plans both small and large by asking the following questions:

- Who needs to be either involved in the planning effort or informed along the way?

- Should there be different levels of involvement, from direct decision making to advisory in nature?

- Whose advice do we want/need relative to our plan?

- Once written, is it clear that a leadership plan is in place across district, school, and classroom levels?

- Is there a communications component of the plan that will be uniformly applied to reach all stakeholders? Will those stakeholders, including the school board, be regularly updated on the plan's progress?

Analysis of Impact

When functioning properly, the assessment system provides data for program evaluation, continuous improvement, and school/district accountability, while also providing teachers, students, and parents the information they need on a daily basis to positively affect learning. Your action plan is a statement about what parts of that system you want to improve. As part of the plan, it is important to document evidence of that improvement.

Professional development programs in classroom assessment may be at the center of many action plans. We recommend that all who implement such programs design and conduct their own local program evaluations. Such evaluations can be both formative and summative. Formative evaluations help program directors monitor and adjust their professional development efforts as they go. Their purpose is program improvement. Summative evaluations provide evidence of effectiveness to those who fund the professional development efforts or who are responsible for their success. These evaluations inform judgments of overall program effectiveness. Evaluators can conduct meaningful evaluations by focusing evidence gathering at any of a variety of levels. Here are two examples, which can be used alone or in combination.

Case Study of an Individual Teacher or a Few Teachers

In-depth study of a small number of teachers can yield descriptions of classroom assessment practices. By watching these teachers' practices grow and change over time, leaders can draw inferences about the impact of professional development programs. Possible questions to consider:

- What effect did the professional development program have on their classroom assessment practices?

- What did these teachers experience in the professional development model?
  — What worked?
  — What did not?

- What did these teachers experience in applying new assessment practices?
  — What worked?
  — What did not?

- What is different in their classrooms now as a result?

Because an evaluation of this sort focuses on understanding a few specific experiences, one can examine in detail how and why the professional development effort worked or didn't. In this case, generalizability of results is sacrificed for depth of understanding.

However, generalizability of results can be enhanced by including teachers from a range of contexts (grade levels and content areas). This kind of evaluation can be conducted by following teachers as they develop assessment literacy. Or, it can center on the teachers' design and implementation of action research studies focused on student-involved classroom assessment (described in the next subsection).

The Study of a Learning Team

A learning team is a structured adult learning experience that relies on collaborative, job-embedded, and hands-on practice-based learning. Another program evaluation approach is to pool the evidence across team members to draw inferences about program impact. The objective is to generate a composite picture of the learning and growth of a group of teachers working together. The strength of this approach is its focus on the effects of collaborative learning. Following are some of the questions these evaluations can address:

- How did the group define success?
- What meeting and learning procedures did they follow?
- Was the time/schedule sufficient and appropriate for learning?
- What were their group norms for interaction?
- Did facilitation at team meetings generate rich discussions about assessment practice?
- What evidence of greater assessment literacy emerged?
- What kinds of teaching changes resulted?
- What was the extent of success and challenges?

In Closing

Through the use of high-quality assessments *of* and *for* learning, linked to the targets of instruction, all students will be able to show what they know and can do. A system that is in balance will ensure that the right kind of assessment is used for the right purpose, and that assessment will be used to continually improve student learning. We have focused the contents of this Action Guide on our belief that strong classroom assessment is the heart of any assessment system.

But it is through a combination of assessments, working in a coordinated fashion, that students can truly prosper and where all information needs can be met. Students can become confident, competent learners. Your work and the work of your colleagues in pursuit of assessment balance and quality will benefit teachers, schools, and communities, but will benefit most especially the students we all serve.

References

Ames, C. (1992). Classrooms: Goals, structures, and student motivation. *Journal of Educational Psychology, 84*, 261–271.

Arter, J. A., & Chappuis, J. (2006). *Creating and recognizing quality rubrics*. Portland, OR: Educational Testing Service.

Atkin, J. M., Black, P., & Coffey, J. (2001). *Classroom assessment and the National Science Standards*. Washington, DC: National Academy Press.

Bandura, A. (1994). Self-efficacy. In V. S. Ramachaudran (Ed.), *Encyclopedia of human behavior* (Vol. 4, pp. 71–81). New York: Academic Press.

Black, P., Harrison, C., Lee, C., Marshall, B., & Wiliam, D. (2002). *Working inside the black box: Assessment for learning in the classroom*. London: King's College.

Black, P., & Wiliam, D. (1998). Inside the black box: Raising standards through classroom assessment. *Phi Delta Kappan, 80*(2), 139–148.

Blanchard, K., & Johnson, S. (1982). *The one-minute manager*. New York: Morrow.

Brown, A. (1994). The advancement of learning. *Educational Researcher, 23*(8), 4–12.

Butler, R. (1988). Enhancing and undermining intrinsic motivation: The effects of task-involving evaluation on interest and performance. *British Journal of Educational Pyschology, 58*, 1–14.

California School Boards Association. (1999). *Targeting student learning: The school board's role as policymaker*. Springfield, IL: Illinois Association of School Boards.

Cameron J., & Pierce, D. P. (1994). Reinforcement, reward, and intrinsic motivation: A meta-analysis. *Review of Educational Research, 64*(3), 363–423.

Chappuis, J. (2007). *Learning team facilitator handbook*. Portland, OR: Educational Testing Service.

Chappuis, J. (2009). *Seven strategies of assessment* for *learning*. Portland, OR: Educational Testing Service.

Chappuis, J., & Chappuis, S. (2002). *Understanding school assessment: A parent and community guide to helping students learn*. Portland, OR: Educational Testing Service.

Collins, J. (2001). *Good to great*. New York: HarperCollins.

Commission on Instructionally Supportive Assessment. (2001). *Building tests to support instruction and accountability*. Arlington, VA: American Association of School Administrators.

Council of Chief State School Officers. (2008). *Educational Leadership Policy Standards: ISLLC 2008. As adopted by the National Policy Board for Educational Administration*. Washington, DC: Author.

Covey, S. (1989). *The seven habits of highly effective people*. New York: Simon & Schuster.

Covington, M. V. (1992). *Making the grade: A self-worth perspective on motivation and school reform*. New York: Cambridge University Press.

Davidovich, R., Nikolay, P., Laugerman, B., & Commodore, C. (2010). *Beyond school improvement: Journey to innovative leadership*. Thousand Oaks, CA: Corwin.

DuFour, R., DuFour, R., Eaker, R., & Karhanek, G. (2004). *Whatever it takes: How professional learning communities respond when kids don't learn*. Bloomington, IN: National Educational Service.

Dweck, C. S. (1999). *Self-theories: Their role in motivation, personality, and development*. Philadelphia: Psychology Press.

Fullan, M. (2001). *Leading in a culture of change*. San Francisco, CA: Jossey-Bass/Wiley.

Fullan, M. (2004). Leadership and sustainability. Presentation given at the Assessment Training Institute, Portland, OR, July 2004.

Fullan, M. (2008). *The six secrets of change: What the best leaders do to help their organizations survive and thrive*. San Francisco, CA: Jossey-Bass/Wiley.

Gladwell, M. (2000). *The tipping point*. Boston: Little, Brown.

Goleman, D., Boyatzis, R., & McKee, A. (2002). *Primal leadership: Realizing the power of emotional intelligence*. Boston, MA: Harvard Business School.

Guskey, T. R. (2002). Computerized gradebooks and the myth of objectivity. *Phi Delta Kappan, 83*(10), 775–780.

Hattie, J., & Timperley, H. (2007). The power of feedback. *Review of Educational Research, 77*(1), 81–112. Retrieved 08 October 2007 from http://rer.sagepub.com/egi/content/full/77/1/81

Jacobs, H. H. (1997). *Mapping the big picture: Integrating curriculum and assessment K–12.* Alexandria, VA: Association for Supervision and Curriculum Development.

Kluger, A. N., & deNisi, A. (1996). The effects of feedback interventions on performance: A historical review, a meta-analysis, and a preliminary feedback intervention theory. *Psychological Bulletin, 119*(2), 254–284.

Knowles, M. (1990). *The adult learner: A neglected species.* Houston, TX: Gulf Publishing.

Leithwood, K., Louis, K., Anderson, S., & Wahlstrom, K. (2004). *How leadership influences student learning.* New York: The Wallace Foundation.

O'Connor, K. (2007). *A repair kit for grading: 15 fixes for broken grades.* Portland, OR: Educational Testing Service.

Office of Superintendent of Public Instruction. (1996). *Designing a district assessment system.* Olympia, WA: Author.

Peters, T., & Waterman, R. (1982). *In search of excellence: Lessons from America's best run companies.* New York: Harper & Row.

Sadler, D. R. (1989). Formative assessment and the design of instructional systems. *Instructional Science, 18*, 119–144.

Schmoker, M. (2002). The real causes of higher achievement. *SEDLetter, 14*(2). Retrieved July 2002 from http://www.sedl.org/pubs/sedletter/v14n02/1.html

Seligman, M. E. P. (1998). *Learned optimism: How to change your mind and your life.* New York: Pocket Books.

Senge, P. (1990). *The fifth discipline.* New York: Doubleday.

Sparks, D. (2003). Change agent: An interview with Michael Fullan. *Journal of Staff Development, 24*(1), 55–58.

Stiggins, R. J. (2008). *An introduction to student-involved assessment FOR learning*, 5th ed. Upper Saddle River, NJ: Merrill/Prentice Hall.

Stiggins, R. J., Arter, J., Chappuis, J., & Chappuis, S. (2006). *Classroom assessment* for *student learning: Doing it right—Using it well*. Portland, OR: Educational Testing Service.

Washington Educational Research Association. (1999; revised 2001). Ethical standards in testing: Test preparation and administration. White paper. University Place, WA: Author.

Waters, T., & Cameron, G. (2007). *The balanced leadership framework: Connecting vision with action*. Denver, CO: Mid-Continent Research for Education and Learning. Retrieved 12 January 2010 from http://www.mcrel.org/product/290/

Waters, T., Marzano, R., & McNulty, B. (2003). *Balanced leadership: What 30 years of research tells us about the effects of leadership on student achievement*. Aurora, CO: Mid-continent Regional Educational Laboratory.

Weinbaum, E. (2008). *Learning about assessment: An evaluation of a ten-state effort to build assessment capacity in high schools*. Philadelphia: Consortium for Policy Research in Education, University of Pennsylvania.

About the Authors

Steve Chappuis

Steve's experience as an educational leader includes being principal at the junior and senior high levels, and as a district assistant superintendent for curriculum and instruction. He has led the development and implementation of a standards-based instructional program that included comprehensive assessment policies and strategic plans. He is a coauthor of *Classroom Assessment* for *Student Learning: Doing It Right—Using It Well* (2006) and *Understanding School Assessment—A Parent and Community Guide to Helping Students Learn* (2002) and numerous journal articles on classroom assessment.

Carol Commodore

Carol Commodore is the founding member of Leadership, Learning and Assessment, LLC. She is also one of the founding members of the Wisconsin Assessment Consortium and an independent consultant with the Pearson Assessment Training Institute of Portland, Oregon. Carol has also served as an assistant superintendent for instruction and a coordinator for assessment and has more than twenty years experience as a classroom teacher, having taught students from kindergarten through graduate school. She has facilitated the development and implementation of a districtwide elementary world language program and a districtwide K–12 standards and balanced assessment program for students. Carol is a coauthor of *The Power of SMART Goals: Using Goals to Improve Student Learning* (2001) and *Beyond School Improvement: Embracing Innovative Leadership* (2010).

Rick Stiggins

Rick Stiggins founded the Assessment Training Institute in 1992 to fulfill the mission of providing teachers and school leaders with the professional development needed to meet their rapidly evolving assessment responsibilities. Rick has authored dozens of articles and books that provide frameworks for teacher assessment expertise and assessment quality. In his work at Pearson Assessment Training Institute, Rick and the ATI team have developed and refined innovative approaches to helping practitioners assess accurately and use assessment results productively to support, not merely monitor, student learning. The learning team approach to inservice professional development pioneered by ATI has been used in schools and districts across the United States and Canada.

CD-ROM/DVD Contents

CD-ROM

Activity 1: Reflecting on the Vision of Excellence in Assessment

Activity 2: Building a Vision of a Quality, Balanced Assessment Program

Activity 3: Formative or Summative?

Activity 4: Conducting an Assessment Audit

Activity 5: School/District Assessment System Self-Evaluation

Activity 6: Merging Local and State Assessment Systems

Activity 7 Auditing for Balance in Classroom Assessment

Activity 8: Embracing the Vision of a Standards-based School

Activity 9: Implementing the Written Curriculum

Activity 10: Deconstructing Standards into Classroom-level Achievement Targets: Practice for School Leaders

Activity 11: Indicators of Sound Classroom Assessment Practice

Activity 12: Analyze Assessments for Clear Targets

Activity 13: Communicating Learning Targets in Student-friendly Language

Activity 14: Assessment for Learning Self-evaluation

Activity 15: A Rubric for Sound Grading Practice

Activity 16: When Grades Don't Match the State Assessment Results

Activity 17: A Standard Cover Letter to Parents

Activity 18: "Is This Responsible?"

Activity 19: Guidelines for Test Preparation and Administration

Activity 20: Supporting Teacher Learning Teams

Activity 21: Discussing Key Assessment Concepts with Faculty

Activity 22: Verifying Teachers' Content Knowledge and Assessment Competence

Activity 23: Should Teachers Be Held Accountable for Assessment Competence through Evaluation?

Activity 24: Using School/District Policies to Support Quality Assessment

Activity 25: A Self-analysis for School Leaders

Activity 26: Making Connections between Leadership Competencies and the Seven Actions

Activity 27: Making Connections between a District's Current Direction and Assessment Literacy

Activity 28: Linking the Ten Assessment Competencies for School Leaders with the 2008 ISLLC Educational Leadership Policy Standards and the Twenty-one Principal Leadership Responsibilities

Action Planning Templates

DVD Presentation

Developing Balanced Assessment Systems: Seven Essential Actions for Schools and Districts